RISE FROM THE ASHES

Leslie,
Thank you for all
you do at LCCC and
for supporting these stories.
Keep rising.

RISE FROM THE ASHES

STORIES OF TRAUMA, RESILIENCE, AND GROWTH FROM THE CHILDREN OF 9/11

PAYTON LYNCH

NEW DEGREE PRESS

RISE FROM THE ASHES

Stories of Trauma, Resilience, and Growth from the Children of 9/11

ISBN   978-1-63730-426-6 *Paperback*

978-1-63730-509-6 *Kindle Ebook*

978-1-63730-510-2 *Ebook*

Consider it pure joy,
whenever you face trials of many kinds
Because you know that the testing of
your faith produces perseverance.

James 1:2–3

CONTENTS

*To my husband Jon. Thank you for persevering
so that I could tell these stories.*

*In memory of my father-in-law Robert Henry Lynch
Jr. and the 2,977 innocent lives we lost that day.*

FOREWORD

My name is Jonathan Robert Lynch, and I'm a 9/11 Surviving Child.

I'm also much more than that. I'm a performer. A craftsman. A Disney junkie. A Harry Potter enthusiast. A dog lover (and cat tolerator). An adventure seeker. A child of God.

Last but not least, I'm the husband to an amazing woman, Payton, who cares deeply about my story and the story of all 9/11 Surviving Children. Stories of loss, trauma, and despair, but also stories of joy, gratitude, and resilience.

My wife has recognized an insightful connection between my resiliency through many challenges and the loss I experienced as a child on 9/11. After twenty years, the heartache has manifested into something else.

With great integrity and empathy, I've watched my wife write this book, interviewing dozens of 9/11 Surviving Children and grief counselors. I've watched her cry as she pours over research and relives the day with her interviewees. This book has taught me so much about myself and all that I share with other 9/11 Surviving Children. Shared tragedy for sure, but shared triumph as well. The intent is not to downplay the loss we all felt that day, but rather to highlight the resilience, long-term healing, hope, and appreciation that may have come from our loss.

Our stories are important. By sharing them, we can invoke empathy in the hearts of others who don't understand and hopefully prevent something like 9/11 from happening ever again. Our stories can also help others going through trauma see that there is hope for them. There is a light at the end of the tunnel, and you are not alone!

INTRODUCTION

———

Where were you on 9/11?

I was in second grade living in Pennsylvania at the time. We weren't picked up early from school like many others, but I do remember arriving home to find my mom glued to the television. I was too young to understand what was going on, but I could recognize by the worry in my mom's voice that it was bad.

Even living only two hours from New York City, I never knew anyone personally impacted by the attacks on 9/11. I had never even visited the city before that. In fact, I remember my dad driving us into New Jersey to see the now Twin Tower-less NYC skyline. You still couldn't get into the city, and the rubble was still smoking.

Do you know anyone who was personally impacted by 9/11?

While most of us know where we were when we heard the news, it's less likely that you are in a community that was directly affected.

It would be years later until I would learn of anyone with a personal connection. I was on a date on the anniversary of 9/11 with my now husband, Jon Lynch. We had started dating in May of that year, so it was our first September together. What I thought was a casual date was actually Jon sharing his story.

His father, Robert Henry Lynch Jr., was the property manager of Two World Trade Center and was killed in the attacks. I was grateful to be seated in the dimly lit Bonefish Grill restaurant when he shared this story because it was difficult to remain stoic. As a child with two living parents, I couldn't imagine losing a parent not to mention losing them in one of the most public, tragic, and violent losses in American history.

I couldn't understand how this man had lived through such trauma in his childhood and could turn into such a kind, compassionate adult. The odds did not seem in his favor. And yet, here he was, leading a successful and joyful life, despite, and maybe because of, the adversity he faced.

Seven years after that 9/11 dinner date, we are happily married. The year 2020 brought many challenges for us. We were experiencing infertility and the loss of a job, two grandparents, and life as we knew it in less than a year. In addition to our personal challenges, 2020 was also the year of the COVID-19 pandemic.

The pandemic is set to go down in the history books as arguably the most devastating and defining moment of this century. In fact, many have described the COVID-19 pandemic as the turning point from a post–9/11 world to a post–COVID-19 world. Both events shaped the nation, if not the entire world, and through them, protocols and standards have been set.

As we've lived through the challenges of 2020, I've seen my husband, Jon, walk through this season with a grateful and hopeful heart. For as long as I've known him, he has adapted through every challenge, and this was no exception.

I used to not be able to figure it out. Why does Jon respond so positively to adversity while I seem to struggle? While Jon is not defined by the tragedy of 9/11, he is certainly shaped by it. Experiencing the trauma of very publicly losing his father has brought immeasurable heartache. However, years later, those challenges have manifested into something else.

I originally thought Jon's resiliency was an anomaly, but as I researched and learned more about others who had a front-row seat to the tragedy that defined a nation, I found that my husband was not alone. In fact, many children who lost a parent on 9/11 are thriving despite their trauma. In my research, I have found that some analysts believe that children who experience trauma in their childhood may have better coping mechanisms than children who don't. This includes Christina Vroman, a mental health counselor who states that "Many individuals who experience a traumatic event endorse positive outcomes such as a newfound appreciation of life, spiritual renewal, and personal growth." (Vroman 2018).

9/11 Surviving Children bring a unique perspective to the mosaic of stories that make up all of those impacted that day. It's a mosaic they'd rather not be a part of, but the breadth of their experiences brings color to the human condition. The impact that their grief has had on their growth has been under-represented in the 9/11 narrative for too long. As we pull back the curtain within these interviews, that's all about to change.

Many of the 9/11 Surviving Children have turned trauma to triumph in their adult years. They've grown up in the shadow of 9/11, and now they're adults, leaving their mark on the world. This isn't just true of 9/11 Surviving Children. I've also had the opportunity to speak with counselors of children who experienced other tragedies, such as the mass shooting at Marjory Stoneman Douglas High School. Many of those children are also experiencing growth after their trauma and contributing to their communities in incredible ways.

Twenty years after 9/11, we are still seeing the results and the consequences in the children who lost a parent that day. As I've been dealing with my own grief, I wondered if there was something all of us could learn about dealing with loss and trauma. What I've learned from the 9/11 Surviving Children has changed not only the way I view 9/11, but also loss in general. It couldn't be timelier as we are all collectively suffering the massive loss that the COVID-19 pandemic has brought to our world.

Throughout this book, we will explore their stories and attempt to uncover the secret sauce to their resiliency. We will dig deeper into what it is that the children of 9/11 can teach us. In doing so, we will also take an intimate dive into the personal challenges that have led me to write this book. On these pages, I've shared the inner musings of my mind as I take the lessons of 9/11 Surviving Children and apply them to my own circumstances. What started first as a project for personal discovery has turned into an opportunity to share what I've learned with all of those walking through grief.

As we look, we will learn where they were on 9/11 and where they are now. After 20 years, we are dealing with completely different challenges than what we suffered through in the midst of 9/11. Still, the common human problem between 9/11 and any other tragedy remains the same: loss, trauma, and violence steal from us, but they can also shape us and make us stronger. The 9/11 Surviving Children remind us that it's what we do moving forward from tragedy that makes a difference.

This book is not just a look back at 9/11, but a glimpse into how the people affected by an enormous tragedy pick up the pieces and move forward. The 9/11 Surviving Children are living proof that all of us can tap into our best selves even after, and sometimes because of, grief and trauma. While you may not have been personally affected by 9/11, we've all experienced loss in some way. The lessons they have to share apply to all of us encountering challenges. In hearing their stories, we will discover what it means to bounce forward after tragedy, and how each of us has the capacity to unlock these skills in our own lives.

THE DAY

———

Jon Lynch. World traveler. Walt Disney World Parade performer.

Rebecca Asaro. FDNY firefighter. One of six siblings.

Thea Trinidad Budgen. A WWE female wrestler.

Pete Davidson. Star on Saturday Night Live. Comedian and actor.

It sounds like the setup to a very bad joke, but not this time. What do they all have in common? Along with my husband, who is included in this list, all of these people are connected by common tragedy. They are the children of 9/11, with each of them losing a parent during the terror attacks that day.

I've only included a few names here. Frankly, I wouldn't have enough room in this book alone to write of every child that lost a parent that day. In fact, over three thousand children lost at least one parent on September 11, 2001 (Meyjes 2019). If you ask the folks at the Tuesday's Children organization, this number rises to five thousand if you count people who were over eighteen at the time. Five thousand people woke up on that seemingly normal Tuesday, not knowing that they'd never see their parent ever again.

This staggering number does not even include the countless others who continue to lose their parents due to 9/11–related illnesses. Due to the amount of toxins that those who were there that day were subject to, those who survived are dying of cancer and other illnesses at an alarming rate. While there is no official count, it is believed that the number of people who have died from 9/11–related illnesses now surpasses the number of people who died that day (Waichman 2020).

To make matters worse, 9/11 survivors who have acquired 9/11–related illnesses seem to be impacted more than the general population by COVID-19. With as many as sixty-eight cancers and dozens more respiratory issues reported by 9/11 survivors, this group is "uniquely vulnerable to an illness that attacks the lungs and the immune system," Patrick Rheaume, spokesperson for New York City attorney Michael Barasch, added (Siemaszko 2020).

This is just one example of how 9/11 still haunts those who were directly impacted. While the rest of the world has moved on, these people continue to feel the repercussions of that day. In many ways, 9/11 has been the catalyst to what feels like endless ripple effects.

I knew that if there was any way to tap into why my husband Jon is so resilient today, I would have to go back much further in time to understand. What happened in between the most devastating day of his life up until now that makes him a stronger person? And are there others that have a similar journey?

I sought to learn more about the 9/11 Surviving Children, interviewing dozens of them and hearing their stories. While I imagined I'd learn a lot about this group of people, I never expected what they'd teach me about myself or even my husband. As they recounted the events of 9/11 as they know them to be, it's as if pieces of their souls were unlocked. Their memories are placed on display for you here, naked and vulnerable for the world to see.

As to not compromise the truth as those I interviewed know it to be, I've documented these elements exactly as they remember them. This could very well mean that the events you read below actually happened out of sequence, in a different timeframe, or slightly altered from how 9/11 Surviving Children remember them.

There is much to unpack as to *why* memory works in this way.

As I've interviewed a few 9/11 Surviving Children and their sibling groups, it is not uncommon for their memories of the day to differ. There are several reasons why this may be true. For siblings old enough to remember on their own, trauma of this kind can often lead to the blocking of memories as a posttraumatic stress disorder (PTSD) response. According to Darlene McLaughlin, MD, psychiatrist, and clinical assistant professor with the Texas A&M College of Medicine, "If the brain registers an overwhelming trauma, then it can essentially block that memory in a process called dissociation—or detachment from reality... The brain will attempt to protect itself," (Texas A&M College of Medicine 2019).

If you've ever daydreamed before, then you've experienced this same dissociation in a milder form. I've seen this happen with my husband as well, who, even though he was thirteen at the time, distinctly recalls memories of 9/11 that either didn't happen, or happened in another sequence or timeframe than what the rest of his family recalls. I tread lightly when bringing up the memory gaps. My husband recalls so passionately what he experienced that day, how could I tell him he's wrong?

For those that don't remember, they are relying on the memories of those who were there to fill in the blanks. And if those they are relying on are having memory blocks, it can be difficult to fill in the pieces. Processing the loss of a loved one is difficult even when all of the information is there. With so many unknowns for those impacted by 9/11, there continues to be significant confusion and hurt associated with that time. Talking to someone about this time, whether personally or professionally, has helped many 9/11 Surviving Children recall and make peace with certain memories.

Together, let's dive deep into the memories of these children as they remember 9/11. There is so much to be learned from the Surviving Children, but we need to start at the beginning.

For most, the morning of 9/11 seemed like any other morning. People went to work and sent their kids to school without a second thought. I think of my own normal, Tuesday mornings as an adult and find it difficult to recount exactly what I do on those days since they are typically just as mundane as the day before. On 9/11, it all seemed unremarkable—until it wasn't.

8:46:40 a.m. EST: Flight 11 crashes into the North Tower of the World Trade Center between the ninety-third and ninety-ninth floors.

Suddenly, this normal morning was anything but. Many on the East Coast of the United States were already where they needed to be for the day by the time the first plane hit.

This meant that kids were finding out about the tragic events unfolding while in their classrooms.

JON LYNCH

On that fateful Tuesday, Jonathan Lynch, eldest son of Robert Henry Lynch Jr., was thirteen years old and sitting in his middle-school art class in Whitehall, Pennsylvania.

"I remember my teacher turning on the television and the first tower was already bleeding smoke. I remember saying, 'My dad works there,' and the teacher giving me a horrified look. He said, 'I hope he's alright,' and left it at that. Living in Pennsylvania, I was the only person in the entire school district who had a parent working at the Trade Center."

Jon's parents were divorced, which is why he was in Pennsylvania during the attacks. He and his oldest sister (in college at the time of 9/11) both lived with their mom there. Their dad, who had been remarried for several years, lived in New Jersey with their stepmom and three half-brothers.

Even at thirteen, Jon had a hard time understanding what he saw on the television screen and what it meant for his dad. "I was an oblivious teenage boy. I don't remember really thinking anything at all until I got a call from the office."

Like many children that day, Jon's mother was coming to pick him up from school early. With his older sister away at school, they needed to pick her up before making the drive out to New Jersey, where his father lived.

"It was about a two and a half hour drive from my mom's house to my dad's. I swear we were the only car on the road that day. And of course, on our way to New Jersey, my mom got pulled over for speeding. I recall my mom yelling at the cop that my father was in the towers and my sister crying in the front seat. The cop let us go immediately."

With all of Jon's family now gathered at his father's home in New Jersey, they found comfort with one another and held on to hope that his father was still alive. Family huddled around the phone and the television. Jon recalls never having seen that many cars in his life outside of the house.

"We knew he was out of the building when the first plane hit because he called the house and left a voicemail. I can still hear his voice in my head, saying 'I'm out of the building, I'm safe. It's bad, it's really, really, really bad. I will call you soon. I love you.'"

After that call, no one in Jon's family dared touch the phone. They wanted to keep the lines open in case they'd hear from their dad again. The family received no calls, and hours turned to days.

"I would watch the news for hours, convinced I saw my dad in the clips. I called my dad's phone, hoping he would pick up instead of getting the dreaded voicemail for the millionth time."

Unfortunately, it was not to be. Weeks went by with no sign of his father, and without any remains to identify him, Jon's family was forced to assume the worst without any real sense of closure. That voicemail home remains in the family collection today, memorializing the last time they heard from their father.

My husband's family alone made up five of those five thousand who lost a parent that day. Each of them, within one day's time, permanently tied together by their tragedy.

MARK LYNCH

As I took on writing this book, it was important to me that my husband's family not feel as if I were taking advantage of them. This topic is a sensitive one, and everyone within Jon's family has different comfort levels with the subject matter. The last thing I wanted was for them to feel exploited the way they have by some news reporters in the past.

I shared with them early on what my intentions were and that I would not ask any of them for interviews unless they pursued me about it. As I reached the end of the interview phase for the book, Jon's youngest brother, Mark Lynch, reached out to me. He wanted to set up a time to talk about his unique experiences with 9/11. I couldn't pass up the opportunity to learn more about my brother-in-law and gain a new perspective within the same family.

Only one year old at the time of 9/11, Mark has no personal memories of the day himself. The reality of this is something that has weighed on Mark throughout his whole life. Like other 9/11 Surviving Children who are too young to remember (and we will talk to a few of them throughout this book, including Cat Brennan, Lex Edwards, and Rose Thomas), this fact doesn't make their stories less important.

For some of those in this age group, the events of 9/11 seem to be somehow separated from the loss of their parent. The event they learn about in their history books has a different—and yet still harrowing—impact on them when compared to their peers who were older on that day. In some ways, it's impossible to understand the enormity of the loss without the "I remember when" moment. And yet, their family trees were greatly impacted by this event before they could even speak. They bring a unique perspective to life as they grew up without any knowledge of a pre-9/11 world.

MATTHEW BOCCHI

Matthew Bocchi, author of *Sway* and son of John Bocchi, remembers the day vividly. His dad, a director at Cantor

Fitzgerald in Tower One, worked on the 105th floor. In his book, *Sway*, Matthew recalls his memories of visiting the office and feeling the buildings shift from the wind.

By 9 a.m., Matthew was pulled out of his fourth-grade classroom. Similar to Jon, Matthew—along with one of his brothers and several other children—was told that something had happened at the World Trade Center, but heard and assumed that everything would be okay. Matthew thought his dad was invincible, and that there was no possible way he could've been hurt.

Soon Matthew and his brother were the only two left in school that day, with all the other children having already been picked up. They rode the bus home to find their entire family and neighbors in their house. There on the television was the constant footage of the terrible morning. Matthew still couldn't believe that anything bad would happen to his dad. He kept calling his father's cellphone, leaving the message, "Come home soon. I love you." Eventually, the phone couldn't hold any more messages.

Matthew would later learn of the several phone calls his family members received from his dad that day. Since his dad was a prankster, Matthew's mom thought that the first call was a sick joke, as John Bocchi told his wife that they think a small plane hit the building before the line cut out. It would take several tries before either one of them would be able to get through again. His final call was to tell her that she was the love of his life.

Even after realizing that his dad was above where the plane hit, Matthew would act out different scenarios of his dad escaping the rubble along with his two younger brothers. This fascination with the events and how they played out that day would soon turn into an unhealthy obsession for Matthew (Bocchi 2021).

THEA TRINIDAD BUDGEN

Matthew and Jon were two of many to have had family members in contact with their parents on that day. At the age of ten, Thea Trinidad Budgen also lost her father. She distinctly remembers her mom getting a phone call from her dad that morning. A call she would not have heard had she been at school, but she was off that day for a doctor's appointment. Even at a young age, she could tell something was wrong.

According to Boon, a journalist at the *US Sun*, Thea could hear her mom pacing downstairs and asked her what was going on.

Her mom had turned on the television, and they watched, horrified—with the Twin Towers already up in flames.

"She was freaking out on the phone and she turns on the television and she says, 'Michael, Michael you're in there?'"

Confused, Thea watched on, and thought that the "Michael" her mom was referring to was her uncle with the same name.

Michael, Thea's father, was calling to say goodbye. Just like Matthew Bocchi's dad, Thea's father worked at the Cantor Fitzgerald firm, and he was trapped on the 103rd floor with the plane underneath him. He told his ex-wife, Thea's mother, that he loved her and to take good care of the kids.

Thea listened on, in disbelief and confusion.

"He didn't know I was there. I could've said, 'Let me speak to him one more time' and I didn't."

The days that followed were a whirlwind of confusion for Thea and her family. Thea was in complete denial and held onto the belief that her dad would come home for several weeks (Boon 2020).

"My dad used to pick me up on the weekends, so (following 9/11), I would still pack my clothes and get ready. After a few weeks, I realized he wasn't coming ... that's when I finally figured it out." (Murphy 2013).

ANNE NELSON

Anne Nelson remembers being in her sixth-grade Cradles of Civilization class when her teacher turned on the television. Anne had just started middle school a few days earlier as she watched the chaos developing less than twenty miles away from her suburban New Jersey town. At eleven years old, Anne was just old enough to understand the gravity of the situation.

"I remember feeling extreme sadness for anyone who was affected, but I knew that my father, Port Authority Police Officer James Nelson, was stationed in Jersey City, New Jersey. Being young and naïve, I had not realized that he would be directed to report to the World Trade Center to assist in the rescue efforts."

Anne took the bus home from school as she had done every other day. But this time was different. Her father wasn't outside the house to greet her as he had done countless times before. Anne's mother, Roseanne, was confused by her husband's absence. She had not been in contact with Anne's father since the morning when he informed her that he was being mobilized to the World Trade Center.

Even though Anne had learned that her dad had gone to the World Trade Center, she still had not processed the fact that her father might not return home.

"I simply thought he was laying in a hospital bed somewhere and would walk through our door once again."

THE THOMAS SISTERS

Ann Thomas—the mother of Mary, Bridget, and Rose—has vivid memories of the day that her young daughters don't have themselves. On a beautiful sunny September morning, Ann walked her two oldest daughters, Mary and Bridget, to school that day. Ann returned home with her youngest daughter, Rose. There they waited for Rose's therapists to arrive. Upon their arrival, they broke the terrible news to Ann.

"When one of the therapists arrived, she said she heard on the radio that a plane just went into one of the Twin Towers. So, we turned on the news."

9:03:02 a.m. EST: Flight 175 crashes into the South Tower of the World Trade Center between the 77th and 85th floors.

"With that, we watched a second plane crash into the second tower. Shortly after our therapy session started, my sister-in-law showed up at my door asking where my husband was. When our meeting ended, I tried calling my husband and his firehouse. I could not get through. My husband worked in Brooklyn, so my thoughts were that there was no way he could have been in Manhattan at those moments."

Unfortunately for Ann and her three daughters, her husband Ted Thomas, along with his brother (both firefighters), were called to the scene. By the next day, they were placed on a confirmed missing list.

These memories of the day, along with all other memories of their father, are moments their youngest—Rose—will never recall. Even her older sisters, Mary and Bridget, only remember bits and pieces of the day. As a Surviving Parent, Ann is able to provide context and color for the day that her young daughters cannot. Her recollection of each moment brings a painful awareness that her daughters will never experience.

Only two years old at the time, Rose has limited memories of the time with their dad. For Rose, the feeling of missing out has continued to challenge her to this day. She says, "I get depressed thinking about it. They have memories of my dad and I don't and I wish I did."

Mary recalls things differently than others in her family. She has heard the tale of being picked up early from school that day but doesn't remember it that way.

"What I do remember distinctly is sitting in the car in the Pathmark parking lot after being picked up from school. I remember the parking spot we were in to this day. My grandma told me a plane drove into a building and that there were firemen and cops there."

Even as her grandma tried to explain what had happened, Mary didn't understand how this would impact her and her family.

For Mary's sister, Bridget, the day is a bit of a blur. She only recalls being in kindergarten that day in the same school as her sister Mary. The family spent a lot of time at Grandma's in the days to follow, something Bridget does recall fondly.

PETE DAVIDSON

Like Mary, Bridget, and Rose, many other firefighter children lost their parents that day. Pete Davidson is a well-known example. Many may know of his rise to comedy fame, but it wasn't until this past year that even I knew of his connection to 9/11. Maybe I've been living under a rock (it's quite possible, as my media consumption ranges from Disney movies to more Disney movies), but until recently, Pete hasn't been as vocal about the loss of his father.

His father, Scott Davidson, was a firefighter at Ladder Company 118 in Brooklyn Heights, New York. He was a firefighter for seven years prior to September 11. Scott was last seen entering the Marriott World Trade Center hotel before the towers collapsed, crushing the nearby building. Pete was only seven at the time.

For firefighter children, they always understood that there was some inherent risk associated with their parent's job. A challenging risk to accept, given it's not the children themselves who sign up for it. And yet, they are the ones who pay the price when something goes wrong. Even with that known risk, many firefighter children did not realize that their parents were at the World Trade Center that day. They assumed they'd be safe and sound.

REBECCA ASARO

For Rebecca Asaro, the realization of all that took place that day in some ways still hasn't sunk in. And yet, the memory of that day is as clear for her as if it were yesterday. Living in New York at the time, Rebecca kissed her dad on the cheek before walking out the door for work. Nine-year-old Rebecca went about the rest of her day as normal, heading off to school. It wasn't until her social studies class that she realized something was wrong.

"Kid after kid kept getting called out of the classroom until there was really no one left. Finally, I was called out and picked up by my mom. We headed to the middle school to pick up my brothers and my mom was really freaking out.

We were listening to the radio, but I still didn't understand what was going on. I didn't even know what the World Trade Center was."

One of six kids, Rebecca and her siblings told stories to rationalize what was happening. Understandably, it was difficult for them to comprehend what a terrorist attack was. They made things up about how the fire started, saying that a few kids pulling a prank had started it. They even told stories about what happened to their dad.

In an effort to preserve the memory of their father and prolong the inevitable, Rebecca's mother made up different stories to explain why he hadn't come home. Ranging from getting lost, to having low blood sugar, the different descriptions of where he might have been remain a point of contention amongst Rebecca and her five other siblings today.

What they know now has been collected over time from the various firefighters their father Carl was with that day. On that morning, Carl was on his way to the towers with two of his Chiefs. After the towers fell, the Chiefs took a record of everyone who was with them that day. That's when they noticed that Carl was missing.

"In October, we had a memorial service at a funeral home. We never found a body. All we had was a PowerPoint of photos to share. We honored his love of the Grateful Dead by playing their songs. Once we made it to the gravesite, we filled his empty casket with the things he loved, like his guitar."

Rebecca shares that this was the first time it really hit her.

"I saw my brothers crying and I realized that he wasn't going to come home."

THE BURNETT SISTERS

Sisters Anna Clare, Halley, and Madison Burnett also received phone calls from their parent that morning. However, unlike many of the 9/11 Surviving Children interviewed for this book, the Burnett sisters were living in California at the time. Their dad called their mother several times on the phone from his flight, United Airlines Flight 93, to say goodbye.

Halley, who along with her twin sister Madison was in kindergarten at the time, remembers more about that day than one might expect. For their family, the morning started like any other. Before school each morning, Halley and her sisters would make their way down the stairs before sunrise to greet their mother, Deena. Their father traveled often, but they could always depend on Deena being downstairs, dressed in her robe, preparing breakfast before the girls headed off to school.

As Halley and her sisters made their way down the stairs that morning, something didn't feel quite right. Halley noticed that there were no lights on other than the glow of the television. Images of explosions and burning buildings flickered their way across the screen. However traumatizing these images might have been, it wasn't the news that caught Halley's attention: it was Deena—dressed in her robe as normal—sitting in her dad's recliner with the landline in her hand. She was on the phone with their dad.

Halley's mother was wailing uncontrollably. She then held out the receiver in front of her, covered the bottom, and cried out "Oh no," over and over again. For Halley and her sisters, seeing their mother in such immense pain is a memory that they'll never forget.

9:28 a.m. EST: United Airlines Flight 93 is hijacked.

The cries of Deena Burnett were in response to the events happening at the other end of the phone. Halley's dad, Thomas Burnett, was telling her that the flight he was on had been hijacked. Deena shared with Thomas what had happened in New York and the Pentagon, and he asked her to call the FBI. Thomas called Deena several times, with Deena continuing to share details of the news as Thomas tried to get a complete picture of what was happening on board the plane.

The last words he spoke to their mother were: "Don't worry. We're going to do something."

Between Thomas and several other passengers on board, they hatched a plan to take over the plane and thwart the hijacker's plot of crashing into another building (many believe it was headed for the US Capitol or White House).

NICOLE FOSTER

Nicole Foster, like many others interviewed for this book, was also very young on the day of 9/11. She was five years old on the day her father died.

"We were headed out the door to swim lessons and my pop pop was sitting in the living room with the television on. That's all I really remember from that day."

It didn't take long for Nicole's house to be swarming with visiting friends and family. The long, winding driveway was full of cars as people arrived to assist Nicole's mom, Nancy. They worked together to put up missing person posters for her dad.

Noel J. Foster, Nicole's dad, was a Vice President with Aon Corporation on the ninety-ninth floor of 2 World Trade. Her dad proved on 9/11 that he was truly always looking to help others. On his final day of work, Noel drove one of his coworkers with a broken leg into the office. Even in his final moments, Noel was helping others.

MARIA GARCIA

Maria Garcia recalls 9/11, but only vaguely. She was nine years old when she lost her dad.

"Some things are very clear while others are very fuzzy and almost non-recallable. One distinct memory I have is sneaking to my bedroom window and waving to my dad, which was something I did almost every morning because he would leave the house at ridiculously early hours."

Living in Long Island, Maria's dad would have to leave early in order to catch the Long Island Rail Road for his commute into the city. This moment that Maria shared with her dad every day would be the last time they would see each other.

From there, Maria's mom got her ready for school as usual. It wasn't until around 10:30 a.m. that Maria realized something might be wrong.

"My sister and I got a call over the loudspeaker to come to the office. They didn't usually call for kids that way."

Maria's mom picked up her sister and her from school and tried to explain what happened. From there, the moments and days become blurry for Maria.

WHY THE DAY MATTERS

Compiling the retellings of the day of 9/11 from the perspective of Surviving Children has been the most challenging part of this journey. The raw details and the feeling of fear that still resonates in their voices as they recall their stories are harrowing moments I'll never forget. These Surviving

Children have likely told their stories more times than they can count. It could have easily become a well-rehearsed show. And yet, the emotions are not gone. Maybe they never go away. And while it's painful to see where the 9/11 Surviving Children have been, it's a crucial step to understanding where they are and, more importantly, where they are going.

Seeing their rock bottom reminds me of my own. While a "misery loves company" approach is not what we are going for, there is a deeper connection between those who have lived and been through the trenches together—even if the experiences differ. The common bond is the grief, pain, and trauma these experiences give us.

No matter who you are, it's likely you've experienced adversity or hardship. And, if you're not in a storm currently, it's likely you should be preparing for one.

The memories of 9/11 for the Surviving Children are important. What's more important is what they do with these experiences. Their next steps inspire us to find the shelter we need from the storms.

RIPPLES

As a wife of a 9/11 Surviving Child, I inherit the baggage of a lifetime of grief. The pebble was thrown into the water that day, and the surrounding ripples continue on, reaching all those that the 9/11 Surviving Children touch. As a person who never knew anyone until my adulthood who lost someone in 9/11, I now live every day feeling its impact.

A prime example of this happened in September 2019 when the doorbell rang and my husband answered to find a mail carrier awaiting his signature to deliver a package. I thought it was a bit weird because it's rare that we ever have to sign for something unless it's a large purchase, so I then wondered what he had bought without telling me! In his hands was a manila envelope with legal documentation inside. More papers to sign. Turns out, a law firm was looking to sue the Kingdom of Saudi Arabia for their involvement with al-Qaeda, the extremist group that executed the attacks on 9/11. (I didn't even know you could sue a whole country; how does that work anyway?) On top of that, I was baffled by the fact that almost twenty years later, there was still paperwork to sign for 9/11–related lawsuits.

In many ways, I've related this reoccurrence and drudging up of old memories to our current challenges with infertility. Over the past two years, my husband and I have struggled to conceive a child. It was something that really took us off guard. No one ever prepared us for infertility. In fact, most of our lives we are told how easy it is to get pregnant and that we should prevent it at all costs. So, when the time was right, we just assumed that things would be easy for us. Unfortunately, we discovered this journey would be anything but.

After about six months of trying, we decided to visit the doctor for a family planning session. We shared that we had been very intentional over the past six months and were concerned that there could be some underlying issues causing our challenges. At first, the doctor was quick to dismiss us. After all, before a certain age, you aren't considered clinically infertile until one full year of trying. Being only twenty-five at the time and in good health, they didn't have any suspicions that I wouldn't be able to conceive. Despite all my efforts to hold back my tears, it was my crying that finally got the doctor to order some lab work for the both of us. While Jon's report came back with seemingly flying colors, mine was less positive. My bloodwork showed signs of elevated prolactin and thyroid-stimulating hormone, both of which can have an impact on fertility. It would take a full year of workups, ranging from extensive genetic testing, bloodwork, dye and saline tests, to finally get a diagnosis of polycystic ovarian syndrome (PCOS). And—while my fertility specialist assures me that it's mild, which is likely why it went uncovered for so long—somehow, I never felt any better having this information.

I was so glad I had trusted my gut and asked for testing, because I was able to begin treatment for these issues.

However, things didn't become easier after that. I quickly became a pin cushion, being constantly stuck with needles every few weeks to see how my hormone levels were responding to medication prescribed by my endocrinologist. When the prolactin levels still wouldn't lower, I had an MRI scheduled to look for a benign tumor, called a prolactinoma, that might be causing the higher levels. I learned very quickly during that MRI that I am claustrophobic. I had to leave and could not complete the procedure on my own.

At this point, I had reached what I thought was rock bottom. I was so angry with the fact that my body couldn't do what it needed to do unmedicated. And now I had to let them shove me in this coffin to check if I had a tumor. Not to mention the fact that we were in the midst of COVID-19 lockdown. I was worried about getting sick every time I visited the doctor or MRI center. Other than that, I hadn't left my house in months. I had been working from home since March of 2020, and Jon was just furloughed (later laid-off) from his dream job at Disney. Fear was at the forefront of everything we did.

I let my mind get the best of me that day, and I lay awake every night until I had to go try for the MRI again. Jon joked that I would put holes in the floor from my constant pacing and efforts to tire myself out before the procedure. This time I was ready with a Xanax prescribed to me to ease my nerves during the scan. Even my mom had to come with me to make sure I didn't back out again. The whole thing felt so defeating.

Soon I became medicated for the prolactinoma, and Jon and I were feeling hopeful. After all, these were the only two things stopping us from getting pregnant, right? And yet, months would come and go, and we would still not conceive. I became the queen of Google, searching for information anywhere of tricks I could try to get pregnant. If there is a wives tail out there you've heard about how to get pregnant—we've tried it. All this coupled with the endless unsolicited feedback from family and friends on what we should be doing, or what worked for their Aunt Suzy. If I had a dollar for every time someone told me to just relax …

Even to this day, no amount of relaxing, or not relaxing, medication, gluten-free/dairy-free/soy-free diet, wearing socks all of the time, acupuncture, and now fertility meds, has enabled us to conceive. My life has been focused all on one thing: getting pregnant. I've lost my identity on this journey. I have felt worthless, and sad, and alone for days on end.

I recently had what I'm experiencing referred to as a lack of gain. But for me, I've always perceived it as a loss. A loss of my plans for a family. A loss of opportunity. A loss of hope.

When you are infertile, each month is a constant reminder of what could have been. When someone dies, there are similar feelings of what has been lost and what could have been. The key difference is that the person doesn't continue to die every single month! There is some amount of closure and peace that comes with time. With infertility, my plans for a family die. Every. Single. Month. Like clockwork, the start of a new cycle will pop up to say, "Hey, remember me? I'm here to crush your spirit again!"

Living with someone who lost a parent in 9/11 can be very similar. While the paperwork is a minor nuisance given the larger impacts of 9/11, it's an example of how even in small ways, 9/11 never really dies. Sure, it's not like my husband and I think about this every moment of every day, but as soon as you think you're in a good place with it, it pops up again to remind you of your pain.

This doesn't even include the yearly routine of needing to avoid all social media and television in early September to self-preserve against the endless videos and pictures of the attacks. Imagine if you lost a family member in a tragic car accident. How would you feel if every year, on the anniversary of their death, people shared a picture of the accident on your Facebook page with the sentiment, "Thinking of you"? This is a harrowing example, but it illustrates the experience for every 9/11 Surviving family member who must sift through the myriad of burning towers images in September of each year. Standing alongside and watching my husband experience these things has been so painful. There are many days I wish I could just make it all go away, but I can't.

My husband Jon has learned to compartmentalize memories of his dad and memories of 9/11. Even today, 9/11 is often brought up in conversation by others around us, none of them the wiser that Jon lost his dad that day. Jon stoically continues the conversation without even a pause. On the flip side, there are days where I can't even see a pregnant woman or the millionth pregnancy announcement without completely breaking down. There are even times where I've been angry with Jon because somehow, he had figured out a healthy way to deal with all of the crap we are going through. I wanted access to this peace, patience, and hope! It was like watching someone eating a big giant bowl of ice cream, knowing they are not sharing, and you're lactose intolerant anyway!

I want the ice cream. I want a huge, heaping bowl of it. I want every bite to fill me with the incredible wisdom and kindness my husband has. So, I keep listening and learning. Because I know this isn't like osmosis. I'm not a flower who will just absorb the rays of these lessons. I am human. And with being human, there is a process that must take place to be able to compartmentalize, realize, express, and understand emotion. I've got work to do, but I'm ready and willing.

THE STORIES

While each set of memories of 9/11 are different, there is a devastating commonality between many of the Surviving Children: a lack of closure. Many of them mention weeks on end of not knowing as being the most vivid and painful memories surrounding that day. There was so much uncertainty that it could be paralyzing. As we live out the impacts of COVID-19, that sense of uncertainty can be felt today. It can be seen in the decision fatigue which is alive and well in a world where we are faced with countless options.

For myself, decision-making wasn't something I struggled with before this year. I could usually envision a clear path forward and what the outcomes of that choice might be. In the midst of a global pandemic, making a choice isn't easy anymore. There is absolutely no way to predict what decision is right because things that felt right before have blown up in our faces. Things that were hard on a normal day are now exacerbated by the isolation we experienced as we quarantined in our homes.

As my husband so eloquently put it, "Our plans this year have sucked and all fallen apart, so what's the point in making any more?"

With this modern context we have after living through a pandemic, it's easy to understand how the 9/11 Surviving Children felt on 9/11 and the days to follow. Their parents had a tough choice to make, with most of their children recalling that their parent intended to make things as normal as possible for their kids. This meant sending them back to school and getting them back into their routines. It couldn't have been easy, but it was these baby steps that kept life moving for children whose entire lives had just been upended.

As I think on my own challenges this past year, I see how—like the children of 9/11—I am in many ways paralyzed with uncertainty. My inner monologue says, "Up to this point, nothing we've tried in our own power has gotten us pregnant, so why would this next thing work?" It's a less-than-graceful attitude that I've brought to the past year. I found myself having 2019 expectations in a 2020 year, which is a lot to ask for, given all the year has thrown at us as a global community. It wasn't until I stepped back that I realized it isn't just the big decisions that lead you to your next destinations. It's the tiny baby steps that keep things moving forward. Sometimes for me, that means getting out of bed in the morning is a good step. Advocating for myself and not crying in front of my doctor is a good step. Taking a break from the fertility drugs and endless tracking is a good step.

It's the baby steps that help us to survive and eventually thrive. But it doesn't happen overnight, and it doesn't happen alone.

For the 9/11 Surviving Children who are leading successful lives now, many of them experienced support from family and friends that helped them walk through this difficult time. It is clear in the countless examples of children who found that their houses were filled with the chatter of friends and family following the attacks.

For anyone who has experienced the death of a loved one before, you know the busyness of this time. Sometimes the constant visits and check-ins from others can be so exhausting that it's almost a welcome relief when the house is finally empty and quiet. And after that, the support seems to do a complete 180 and cliff dive.

Much can be attributed to the support of friends and family that transcended the time immediately following the attacks. These family and friends provided support and guidance that have been essential to the growth of 9/11 Surviving Children. In many ways, it is the surrounding support group that helped these kids—now adults—memorialize their parents.

While the 9/11 Surviving Children have many things in common, you may have picked up on the fact that those spoken to in this book all lost fathers that day. This was something I myself didn't realize until it was pointed out to me. It wasn't intentional at all, but was rather a product of those who reached out and felt comfortable having their stories told. This made me wonder why there are so many children who lost fathers, and where are the people who lost mothers that day?

What I found is that the number of men who died on 9/11 is significantly higher than the number of women. According to NY Mag, the ratio is 3:1 (NY Mag 2014). There are many reasons why we could speculate that this is the case. We have to remember that this was 2001, and many of the World Trade Center jobs and even first responder jobs were traditionally filled by men at the time (a debate and conversation for another day!).

While there are certainly significant stories and lessons to be heard from those who lost mothers that day, there is something to be said about the strength of mothers of children who lost fathers; I don't think it's a coincidence that it was their children who reached out for this project.

We heard from 9/11 Surviving Children in the recollections of the day how their Surviving Parents stepped up despite their own grief. This demonstrates the immense impact these Surviving Mothers had on their children on their paths to recovery. According to Stacie Boyar, a Licensed Mental Health Counselor in Coral Springs, Florida, establishing a routine and sticking to it is extremely impactful for children undergoing trauma.

"Children need to see that they have stability from those who remain to provide comfort to them."

While this book focuses exclusively on the 9/11 Surviving Children, these statements on the importance of strong parenting after experiencing a loss have me thinking about all the parents who lost a spouse that day. I think of Ann, the mother of the Thomas sisters, who kept the plates all spinning. I think of Jon's mother and stepmother, who persevered and provided a sense of normalcy (if that's even possible during that time) for their children, all while struggling through their own loss. How do resilient people get up each day when it feels impossible? They put one foot in front of the other. They take baby steps. And they remember that their loved one would want them to keep moving forward. Because of their determination, they raised a kinder and more resilient generation of children.

Humans are meant to be together in community. We were designed for it. We long for it. Many 9/11 Surviving Families found it. I want to find it. I want you all to find it, too.

Even for my husband, Jon, who was old enough to remember his dad, there are pieces to the puzzle of who his dad was that are unlocked when speaking to others who knew him. From these interactions, we have the stories of their parents that the 9/11 Surviving Children cherish.

Uncovering the details of what happened to their parents on 9/11 was visibly painful for many of the 9/11 Surviving Children I spoke with. I purposely started most of my interviews focusing on that as a means of "getting it out of the way." What I found, interweaved in those retellings, was a glimmer of hope when they spoke about who their parent was. I wanted to tap into that happy place with all of them, so I asked them to share more of the stories they remember or have heard about their parents. It's in these spaces of their minds that their parents live on. While many of these stories include happier memories, I thought there might be another reason why they seemed to bring the 9/11 Surviving Children so much joy. Even though they recognized the fact that they were talking about someone they'd never have this time with again, the nostalgia seemed to put them in a blissful fog, like a haze of comfort wrapping them up into their memories.

Currently in the midst of my own struggle, I don't look fondly on the stories I have to tell. I'd very much rather not have to tell them. I had a feeling there might be something about the amount of time 9/11 Surviving Children have had, and their ability to make peace with the memories of their loved ones.

THE SCIENCE BEHIND TELLING STORIES

Science seems to back up what the 9/11 Surviving Children already know: preserving the memories of loved ones helps families find a way through their grief. According to Greg

Adams, director of the Center for Good Mourning at Arkansas Children Hospital in Little Rock, "One of the most powerful and effective ways of keeping someone's memory alive is talking about them and referencing the person in daily life and conversation. It doesn't have to be a special occasion or an especially emotional time. We can remember and talk about the person anytime."

This can be more difficult in the beginning as memories bring both pain and comfort. Adams says, "In the beginning after a loss, pain often takes center stage and it can be hard to feel comforted by memories. The pain may not ever fade away, but it can move 'backstage' and allow for more experiences of comfort and gratitude."

Adams also shares that "most people find comfort in remembering someone by having a 'memory object'—a belonging of the person who died that is now kept by someone who cared for that person." For those who hold tight to them, "memory objects have value far beyond their material and can be a great source of stories, memories, connection and comfort." (Lanford 2014).

Throughout these stories, we will identify how twenty years of time have paved the way for these memories to bring comfort. We'll also explore the ways in which memory objects impact the 9/11 Surviving Children. This analysis can help us to find strength in our own stories and own the things that bring us comfort.

JON LYNCH

Despite the horror that allowed these attacks to happen, stories of heroism on that day are plentiful. While some of Jon's stories are of his own recollection, many of them are of what he came to know about his dad from the others who crossed his path on 9/11. It would take years for Jon and his family to know the true impact his dad's actions had on that day.

"As property manager of one of the buildings, everyone knew my dad. This made it easier to talk to others after the attacks and pinpoint his location throughout the day."

For weeks following the attacks, Jon's family couldn't understand how he went from outside and safe to becoming one of the victims.

"Friends and coworkers shared stories of my dad leading people out of the building. His last known location was on the escalator in the main lobby."

Through the memories of those who were with him that day, Jon learned that his dad went back into the building to save others.

For his act of heroism, Jon's father, along with 442 others, received the 9/11 Heroes Medal of Valor, created specifically for public safety officers who were killed on that day. The families accepted the medal for their loved ones from President George W. Bush on the White House Lawn on September 9, 2005.

"My dad was not a public safety officer, he was a civilian, and was still honored as a first responder for his sacrifice."

Jon often jokes that he still isn't sure what his dad actually did for a living at the World Trade Center. His dad would take him to work often and recalls everyone knowing him by name. His memories are full of fun days in NYC—shopping, eating pizza, skating in Central Park, Yankee games, and going to the World Trade Center Observation Deck. One of his fondest memories is how fast the elevators were.

"We would ride the elevators from the bottom to the top. We would jump before we got to the top floor and, weightless, we would soar into the air."

The joy in Jon's voice when he shares these memories is infectious. The way his eyes light up and his arms flail about as he mimics the feeling of weightlessness on the elevators is a sight to see. I wish I could bottle these memories up for him in a jar and access them whenever he's feeling sad or missing his dad.

A collector by nature, Jon also finds great comfort in memory objects.

"I was at Camp Hope and we were asked to bring shirts that belonged to our parents to make into pillows. I remember distinctly knowing which shirts I would want to use. I remembered my dad wearing them, they even smelled like him. Today I treasure that pillow, along with the many other things I have that belonged to him."

The key to memory objects is that they mean the most to people who remember the person before they died. Having a few of his dad's favorite items is an important way for Jon to feel close to his dad. He holds as tightly to that pillow he made as he does the stories and memories of his dad.

MARK LYNCH

Mark's understanding of who his dad was is made up of what others have told him. I think Mark has easily heard the elevator story from Jon at least a million times. At least, I've *heard* Jon tell this story to his brother this many times, and I can only imagine how many actual times he's told it.

As big brother, Jon feels it's his duty to share what he knows with him. When Mark talks about his dad, he remembers him as a kind, generous person who was always willing to help.

After 9/11, Jon and Mark's family received several letters from people who knew their dad, which helped Mark to form a mental picture of who this man must have been. They included stories that exemplify his personable demeanor. Today, these letters are bound together in a single book memorializing him.

The book includes memories from his high school buddies, from goofing off together to working on cars. There is one letter that gives an incredible glimpse into the type of person their dad was. It was written by two complete strangers he had met on the train on the way home from work.

Riding the train was an activity he did regularly as a part of his commute to and from the city. This time, he was headed home with a massive telescope, a gift for his kids. While there, he met a couple who were visiting New York for the first time. The telescope caught their eye, and they began to engage in conversation. He told them about his job at the World Trade Center and all the wonderful places they should visit during their stay. Before he left, he gave them his card and told them to reach out the next time they were in the city. He had made such a lasting impression on these people that when 9/11 happened, they looked up his name to see if he was on the missing list. To their dismay, he was, and so they wrote a letter sharing this sweet, fleeting memory with his family.

These stories have a lot of significance for Mark, especially since comfort objects hold much less significance for him than they do his brother Jon. Mark can find it challenging to make connections with his father's belongings because he doesn't have his own personal memories of his dad wearing or using these objects.

He shares, "My brother has a shirt that he says was Dad's and while I think that's cool and all, it doesn't do anything for me."

Where Mark has connected is with the items that relate to hobbies and interests that he has today. Mark has held on to several boxes of mint-condition classic comic books from his dad. As a comic book lover himself, Mark finds comfort in the bond he feels with his dad based on this common interest.

ALEXA EDWARDS

Dennis Edwards, Alexa's father, was thirty-five years old and a partner at Cantor Fitzgerald at the time of 9/11. He was fondly called "The Mayor" because everyone seemed to know and love him. Alexa lights up as she shares about her dad, whose engaging personality is admired by so many. It seems that she is in many ways proud of the man she never had the chance to know.

Alexa clings to the home videos and the relationship she holds with her dad's friends and family as they unlock the moments with her dad that she cannot remember herself. Before he passed, Alexa's dad could be found curled up with her, reading her a book every night before bed. This routine was one that he cherished and something Alexa's mother may have taken for granted.

When we have someone with us every single day, it's easy to forget the little things they do, such as the daily tasks they take care of that we don't even know about. We become dependent and expectant on one another, and then struggle to know where to start picking up the pieces when they are gone.

After he died, Alexa's mom had a hard time filling that gap. Not because she didn't have time or skill to read the books (in fact, she was reading the books very well!). The problem was that Alexa's dad used to make up the stories as he went along, rather than reading off of the pages. Alexa would protest, saying, "That's not how Daddy read them!", which would break her mom's already fragile heart.

Luckily for Alexa, her mom maintained a good relationship with her dad's family and friends. If Alexa's mom had never maintained those relationships, Alexa might never have had access to these stories of her dad. Time and time again, we see how the surviving parent made sacrifices for their children so that they might prosper. It could not have been easy for Alexa's mom to be surrounded by the family that reminds her of all she lost. And yet, she made sure that Alexa would have access to the support system she needed. This community assures Alexa that she shares many personality traits with her dad, including her outgoing personality and willingness to help.

How willing was her dad to help? Eight years prior to 9/11, during the World Trade Center bombing, he helped carry a pregnant woman down eighty flights of stairs. Because of acts like this, Dennis's family knew in their guts that he was not going to escape 9/11 alive. He would be inside, helping others, just as he had always done. The gravity of this realization, as well as the pride of knowing what kind of person her dad was, wells up inside of Alexa when she speaks about him.

THE BURNETT SISTERS

The Burnett sisters were also too young to understand the impact that their father had on 9/11. Ripped out of their routines, Anna Clare, Halley, and Madison were thrust into the spotlight, finding themselves interviewed and honored by the likes of Oprah Winfrey and George W. Bush. As three young girls, they couldn't possibly understand why they were being interviewed so much. What they understood was that their father was not here anymore, and that he was being honored as a hero.

The reality for many 9/11 Surviving Children is that their parents were directly in the line of fire that day and stepped in however they could to help. Even with the recognition that their parents died saving others, the memories associated with 9/11 are very painful. Instead of focusing on the day itself, many 9/11 Surviving Children recall memories of their parents before the attacks and find ways to memorialize them.

The Burnett sisters had limited time with their dad even when he was alive. Tom Burnett traveled often for work, which made his time with family that much more precious. They cling to a few fleeting memories of their days with dad that make them smile to this day. Tom made it a routine with his daughters when he was home to dance with them before bedtime. Like clockwork, they made their way around their home, Tom throwing his daughters into the air and twirling them around to Wynonna Judd's "I Can't Wait to Meet You."

The memory is an emotional one for Halley as she finds the significance in that song in relation to her father's death.

Halley seemed transported in time when recalling these dances with her dad. While she was "virtually" present, staring back at me in our Zoom call, there seemed to be a warm glaze over her eyes. I think if she could, she'd crawl right back into that memory and take one last dance.

Devout in their faith, Halley and her family take comfort in the fact their dad is now flying high with the Lord that their dad couldn't wait to meet, but never imagined he would meet so soon.

REBECCA ASARO

Rebecca fondly remembers her dad as the life of the party, always throwing barbecues and looking for an excuse to celebrate.

"He loved to cook and he loved to play music, and barbecues were the perfect opportunity to do both."

A thirty-nine-year-old firefighter at the Ninth Battalion in Manhattan, Carl Asaro was a self-proclaimed "Deadhead." Carl loved the Grateful Dead and even threw a memorial party after Jerry Garcia, lead singer of the Grateful Dead, died in 1995.

Carl was an aide at Division 3 on 9/11. When the second plane hit the World Trade Center, he responded with two other chiefs. Before running out the door and into the trucks, a friend turned to Carl and reminded him to take something with him to eat on the road.

"She knew he was a diabetic and didn't want his blood sugar to drop," Rebecca said with a slight smile.

That's the kind of community Carl found himself in as a firefighter. A tight-knit group who had one another's backs.

Rebecca mentions that the love her mom and dad had for one another was an amazing example of marriage. Her childhood holds memories of them being happily married and doting over each other. She mentioned this as a reminder of the kind of marriage she hopes to someday have.

Rebecca takes pride in remembering her dad for all he did that day. For her, his choice in profession and the acts of walking into those burning buildings are all the proof she needs that he is a hero. His firefighting days inspired not only her, but many of her brothers as well, to want to walk in his footsteps. Because of this, in 2018, Rebecca began the process to become a FDNY firefighter. The process was intense, including written and physical exams, along with various other activities during her time in the academy.

Despite wanting to honor her father, Rebecca didn't always know she wanted to be a firefighter. As she looked for ways to give back to her community, she originally was looking to take a career in the medical field until her uncle, also a firefighter, suggested she consider it for herself.

Rebecca decided it was worth a shot to take the exam and just see what happens. Having done this on a whim without truly taking it seriously, Rebecca was blown away when she received the exam results.

"I passed the test, and I'm so glad I did. It's the best job in the world."

While Rebecca might have been surprised by the results, I certainly wasn't. It only took a few minutes of chatting with her to see how her passion for honoring her father's memory by actively helping others was bound to land her in an incredible career.

THE THOMAS SISTERS

Mary, Bridget, and Rose have many ways, large and small, that they remember their dad. When they played on sports teams as kids, they would take their dad's football number (#85) for their own jerseys. Their family continues to watch old home movies with their dad in them and displays his photos.

Without memories of her own, Rose has to rely on photos and home videos of her short time with her dad.

"My favorite was a game that my Dad called 'Rose-orobics.' He would put me on his head and move me all around and just do crazy things. That video always makes me laugh. I don't have memories, but I do have photos and videos of us together that I hold on to."

Even for Bridget, it's hard to distinguish which memories are from her own mind or from home videos. She fondly recalls wanting to be by her dad's side all the time, washing the car with him and trying to keep up with him and her older sister, Mary.

"My aunt was a hairstylist and would come over to cut our hair. I would always watch her do it. We have a home video where he is sitting on the couch and I'm climbing on the couch. We had these fake scissors for kids, but they didn't cut at all. I wanted to pretend I was a hairdresser, so I went up behind him and cut his hair, and he jumped up so fast because he thought I really did it! It's just little things like that I remember us doing together."

Just retelling this story had Bridget in a belly laugh. I could see how comforting this moment was for her to resurface.

The family continues to stay in touch with their dad's family, celebrating Christmas Eve together and burning two candles throughout the night for their father and his brother who was also lost on 9/11. These bonds, which could have easily been severed after the traumatic loss of their dad, continue to be the glue that keeps his memory alive.

NICOLE FOSTER

Even without many memories of 9/11 itself, Nicole Foster recalls her dad from her early memories.

"I'll never forget this one time we were driving down to the shore. We had about an hour drive, and it was before the days of DVD players in cars. My dad made a built-in television for the car with a VCR for my sister and I to watch our favorite movies. He was just such an easygoing and loving guy. He was always looking to help somebody."

This small act with the VCR, as well as his bravery to help his injured coworker on 9/11, gives us a glimpse of the helpful person Noel was.

As an adult, Nicole has been able to connect with family and friends of her dad's, who share their memories and stories with her.

"A year before my dad died, my sister had to have surgery at Columbia Presbyterian Hospital. My mom told me recently that when they were there, they met another family whose child was also having surgery. They were from the Midwest, and it was their first time in New York City. My dad was talking to them, and they were planning to do all these things in New York. My dad said, 'Don't spend the money on the tourist attractions, just come to my office and you'll be able to see all of New York from the World Trade Center."

Some stories are smaller, but still significant.

"My cousin who is now in his thirties and has two little kids once said that when he was in high school, my dad would watch his band play."

These memories, while they seem like tiny moments in the greater span of time, are what make Nicole feel closer to her dad. In addition, it creates a bond between her and those around her who still fondly remember him.

After moving into a new house, Nicole and her family uncovered more memories that would impact her life in ways she could never imagine. A set of journals that her dad had written about his own childhood showed up when the family was cleaning out their old house. At age four, Noel's father died, a striking parallel to the children he eventually left behind. In order to handle his grief, he wrote down his struggles within those pages and spoke about the parent he'd like to become for his own children.

"To know that my dad could relate to my own set of circumstances was very comforting. There aren't many others who can do that, but through being vulnerable and sharing my own story, I've seen that others want to learn, and there is a sense of common humanity there."

Sharing stories has been a large part of the healing process for her as well as many other 9/11 Surviving Children. Nicole mentions that many of her friends, while they didn't lose a parent in 9/11, have tragic pasts that connect them.

"Even if we're not talking specifically about those events, our challenges bring us closer to one another."

ANNE NELSON

Anne Nelson has many memories of, and with, her father, something many 9/11 Surviving Children—including her sister—do not have.

James Nelson was forty at the time of 9/11. He had worked for the Port Authority Police Department for sixteen years. James had been involved in many other close calls in the past, receiving an award for commendable service performed during a major bus accident. Ironically, the date of that accident was September 11, 1989. James also rescued many during the 1993 World Trade Center bombing, risking his life amongst the black smoke pouring out of the building, despite his asthma. He was also awarded a meritorious police duty medal for his bravery and exceptional work.

"My father was an extremely hard worker. He was a dedicated police officer who was well respected by his recruits and coworkers. He earned a job doing something that he loved, which inspired me not to allow my own share of tragedy to stop me from achieving my goals."

Anne remembers her father as a passionate family man. James had lost both of his parents by the time he was eighteen, which required him to mature quickly and encouraged him to go into police work. He hoped to be the parent to his children that he never had the chance to have.

"When he returned home from work each day, he would playfully toss my younger sister and I onto a bed. I would eagerly anticipate these moments. He coached my youth sports teams and hoped to do the same for my sister when she was older. I especially miss his bear hugs and butterfly kisses. I miss all of those moments terribly."

After the loss of her father, Anne hesitantly learned how difficult it is to let go of something and how that makes her want to tightly latch on to family and friends. Through her practices of gratitude, her relationships with family and friends have strengthened and deepened.

Anne has kept several items that remind her of her father: a pillow made of her dad's clothing, pictures of her dad and her, and the patch and pin from his uniform.

Anne and her sister have both read names of the 9/11 victims at Ground Zero on separate years. The street that Anne grew up on has been renamed in her father's memory. A memorial in her town was named James Nelson Park, along with the softball fields where he used to coach Anne's softball team are now named Nelson Field. There is also a large bronze badge displayed outside of the Port Authority Police command building located near the Goethals Bridge. Her dad, who was stationed at the Staten Island bridges, was honored with a ceremony from the department where they dedicated the badge with her father's badge number in memory of him. These are just some of the ways that Anne memorializes her dad.

"I just never want him to be forgotten. And it's nice that all of these ways keep his memory alive."

For Anne, her memories of her father have reminded her of the person he was, and the person she wants to be.

"A lot of the things I do in my life and the morals I live by are because he instilled them in me. Because of his memory, I remember to not judge a book by its cover and to always do unto others as you would have them do unto you. I try to live by these."

MARIA GARCIA

For Maria Garcia, her dad is present in the people and things around her. Most times, preserving her dad's memory is less intentional than it is an organic part of her life. Oftentimes, Maria will interact with her siblings and find their mannerisms to be just like her dad's.

"The crazy part is that my youngest sister was a baby when my dad died, so the fact that she inherited so many of his traits is cool to me."

There are a few memories for Maria where she can distinctly recall a connection with her dad which led to a passion in her life.

Maria's dad was an avid photographer, which has led to her own interest in the subject. Unfortunately for Maria, this has also meant that her dad was often behind the camera, leaving her with limited photos to remember him by. She is left with her own memories of his interests and hobbies.

Maria is constantly finding out more ways that her and her dad are alike. She stumbled upon his music collection one day, a rack of CDs sitting untouched at her mom's house.

To Maria's surprise, much of the music he collected were bands that she listens to today. It does seem that some of the interests Maria acquired are just a part of her DNA.

"I look at his taste in music and it's fascinating how much overlap there is just accidentally. His CD collection includes Metallica, Pink Floyd, Billy Joel, and some really obscure punk bands that I listen to now. It's not that he exposed me to it, it just worked out that it happened to be the music that I like the most."

CAT BRENNAN

For 9/11 Surviving Children who were too young to remember their parent, the ways of feeling close to their parent are less tangible. Since Cat Brennan was only eighteen months old when she lost her dad, it's tough for her to identify with items of his. Her experiences reminded me of my conversation with my brother-in-law Mark Lynch on comfort objects.

"Sometimes I feel guilty that his things don't mean more to me. It's just that I don't associate these objects with him. For me, I find ways to memorialize my dad wherever I go. It isn't tied to a place or an object."

An interesting finding amongst the children of 9/11 who don't remember their parent is the impact their living parent had on them. For Cat Brennan, who has no memories of her dad, she shares stories of her mom's strength that have helped her become the strong woman she is today.

"I often joke around, asking how it's possible I turned out 'normal,' and I attribute a lot of that to my mom's strength. She kept us going and took care of everything. I know that I'm successful today because of the role model I've had in her. I think on one hand I am very privileged to have been too young to

understand what was happening during 9/11, and thus some-
what sheltered from grief at the time. However, I think being
so young also has allowed me to suppress and ignore a lot of
grief and feelings that have manifested themselves in other
ways which I am honestly only just starting to work through
as an adult. It is sort of like I have just pushed off the grieving
process until I was old enough to truly start to understand the
implications of such a tragedy in my life."

Cat also shares how being raised in a home that openly spoke about her dad has helped her to fill in the gaps of her own memory.

"My mom always answered our questions and people are always telling stories about my dad. We also come up with fun ways to remember him. For instance, on the anniversary of 9/11, my brother and I always have a breakfast of Oreos and milk. I don't know how that started, but it's something I now look forward to each year."

While it's clear that there is no one way to memorialize someone or something after a loss, it does seem that doing so at all has some healing properties.

One good way Greg Adams recommends memorializing someone is to be very intentional about it: "It can be helpful to repeat memorial activities on a regular basis. A caution is not to make a memorial activity too rigid where there is no allowance for change and adjustment as time passes and life changes." (Lanford 2014).

In my current walk with continued infertility, every month feels like a loss. While I was initially hesitant to do so, I purchased an item that I plan on giving my husband when we do someday find out we are having a child of our own. This item helps me to mourn the loss of the babies that will never be, as well as remain hopeful for the child that will someday be.

Whether it's honoring them with Oreos and milk, clinging tight to the badge of their police-officer parent, or thinking hopefully of the day I'll tell Jon we're pregnant, the sentiment is the same. These stories, rituals, routines, and items are a crucial part of activating the happiest thoughts of those we love.

BEAUTY FOR ASHES

It's these happiest thoughts that get me through the less-than-happy moments. For instance, when I woke up one Valentine's Day and realized that my period was now two days late. I had a friend who found out she was pregnant on Valentine's Day two years prior, and I couldn't help but think maybe I could be pregnant too. I was also excited to think that this would mean I would have an October baby—my favorite month. These are the types of spiraling rabbit holes my brain likes to go down every single month.

I had been really good about not taking any pregnancy tests over the past few months. Despite Jon's initially good report, we were eventually diagnosed with dual-factor infertility. This diagnosis encouraged us to move forward with intrauterine insemination (IUI). Since making the decision, I had been feeling more relaxed and at peace with the fact that we may need some additional help with getting pregnant. Still, I had this glimmer of hope remaining that maybe, just maybe, we could get pregnant on our own.

So, against my better judgement, I took a test out from the cabinet, locked the bathroom door, and feverishly attempted to open the box. A few minutes later, I wished I hadn't. One sad, lonely line made its way across the test to tell me that I was yet again, not pregnant. I spent the next hour crying—no—wailing, in the bathroom. Not only was I heartbroken by yet another negative test, but I was angry with myself for being upset. I had been doing so well! What happened?

I am one who is quick to judge how I am feeling about the pain I am experiencing, which has only made my road to recovery that much more challenging. Especially with people constantly telling me to "just relax," I find there are feelings of shame when I'm not feeling relaxed or joyful. Don't people realize that if I could just be happy, I would? I'm not actively choosing to be one way or the other. But when my emotions overcome me, I cannot ignore them.

According to Relief Central, "Acute Grief Reactions are likely to be intense and prevalent among those who have suffered the death of a loved one or close friend. They may feel sadness and anger over the death, guilt over not having been able to prevent the death, regret about not providing comfort, or having a proper leave-taking, missing the deceased, and wishing for reunion (including dreams of seeing the person again). Although painful to experience at first, grief reactions are healthy responses that reflect the significance of the death. Over time, grief reactions tend to include more pleasant thoughts and activities, such as telling positive stories about a loved one, and comforting ways of remembering him/her." (Unbound Medicine 2020).

Grief does not happen in a straight line. It is often one step forward, two steps back. The grief reactions are painful, but very normal parts of the journey. The silver lining is that over time, these grief reactions bring more feelings of comfort than pain. This feeling of comfort is what I see in the eyes of the 9/11 Surviving Children I've spoken with. Time doesn't heal all, but it gives us the space to look back and see what a gift the time they did have was. Holding on to these stories of their parents has played an incredible role in shaping the children of 9/11 into the adults they are today. As many of them mention, sharing their stories helps them to preserve the memory of their parent.

I'm not quite there yet, but seeing into the lives of those who have already been there and have come through to the other side, I know that it's possible for me too.

THE TRAUMA

———

When I spoke with the 9/11 Surviving Children interviewed for this book, I expected them to tell me that their memories and the retellings of 9/11, the day, would be the most traumatic of their lives. It turns out that the years following 9/11 happen to hold some of the most challenging moments. While families still grapple with the loss of their loved ones even to this day, they've developed the skills and wisdom of two decades to guide them through. In the first few years that followed, the path wasn't as clear, and the pain was at the forefront of their minds.

Still, I was stumped as to why the next five to ten years following 9/11 seemed to be just as, if not more, challenging as 9/11 itself. Was the wound still so fresh at that time? Did the support of their family and friends take a cliff dive after the first few years? Through these interviews, we explore the trauma that 9/11 Surviving Children experienced in the days and years following 9/11.

Uncovering how the most traumatic parts of 9/11 Surviving Children's lives played out helps us to understand the reasons for their resilience. With childhood already being such a turbulent time, throwing a trauma on top for good measure was sure to complicate things. And yet, there is something so unique about children who have experienced trauma.

I thought that the way the 9/11 Surviving Children's stories have played out—taking the worst moments and finding the light in them—must be connected in some way. I began to research the subject, learning about what it is that makes children who experience trauma more resilient. What I found is that children with childhood trauma often exhibit higher emotional intelligence as a result of being exposed to challenging times. In fact, a study conducted by Dr. David M. Greenberg and Simon Baron-Cohen found that "adults who reported experiencing a traumatic event in childhood had elevated empathy levels compared to adults who did not experience a traumatic event." (Greenberg, Baron-Cohen, Rosenberg, Fonagy, Rentfrow 2018)

This is good news for 9/11 Surviving Children, because according to Tominey, O'Byron, Rivers, and Shapses in the Young Children publication, "Children with higher emotional intelligence are better able to pay attention, are more engaged in school, have more positive relationships, and are more empathic (Raver, Garner, & Smith-Donald 2007; Eggum et al. 2011). They also regulate their behaviors better and earn higher grades (Rivers et al. 2012). For adults, higher emotional intelligence is linked to better relationships, more positive feelings about work, and, for teachers in particular, lower job-related stress and burnout (Brackett, Rivers, & Salovey 2011)." (Tominey, O'Byron, Rivers, and Shapses 2017).

Knowing the purpose for sharing the trauma—in this case, to unlock empathy in ourselves following our own challenges—made stepping into these painful interviews a bit more bearable for me. I hope that you'll bring the same lens with you as you discover the "rock bottom" for these 9/11 Surviving Children. Remember that these traumatic moments are not the end, just a means to an end.

JON LYNCH

My husband Jon had his fair share of challenging moments. From the constant replay of 9/11 footage on television and in his own mind, Jon has very clear memories of the pain he experienced in the years following this tragic event. Even more notable may be Jon's navigation through the countless difficult conversations he encountered throughout his childhood about 9/11.

Even today, I think of how interested people are in my husband's story. Whenever we tell people that Jon lost his dad in 9/11, they're in shock. Once the initial shock wears off, they tend to go through the same stages of grief that Jon must have gone through over the past twenty years. For Jon, it's another chance for him to tell his and his dad's story. Suddenly, they become a part of something that feels like Six Degrees of Kevin Bacon. Even though we all watched 9/11 with disbelief on our television screens, people living outside of the tri-state area never imagine meeting someone who lost a parent that day. When Jon opens up, his audience suddenly feels like they are a part of some exclusive club.

And while their sympathy is appreciated, there is a gift that comes with anonymity that many 9/11 children do not have. Since Jon was the only person in his entire school district to lose a parent that day, he quickly became the "9/11 kid." This meant that no one really knew what to do with him or how to react. Jon would hear things from well-meaning people that were quite detrimental to his mental health.

"I was told that that anyone who hadn't been identified just picked up and left their lives: changed their names, found new careers, and abandoned their families. I know my dad would never have done that, but it kept me wondering. I would see footage of the attacks on television and imagine that I saw my dad there, or I'd be walking down the street and see someone that looked exactly like him."

Shockingly, even the people Jon should have been able to count on said some of the most challenging things to hear. This includes the less-than-helpful visits to the guidance counselor that Jon suffered through. A scrawny thirteen-year-old at the time, I imagine his little legs swinging from the chair in the office. The bowl of Reese's Sticks the counselor kept on the table seemed to be the most comforting item in the whole room. As he would methodically unwrap the treat from its package, his own guidance counselor would share her theories on what might have happened to his dad. She even suggested it was possible his father was alive in an air pocket for weeks following 9/11.

This dreadful memory of his guidance counselor is one he often shares with others to give them a glimpse into his past. It's always met with the same dropped jaw I had when he told me. "How on earth could a person say that to a kid?" is often the direction the conversation goes next. The reality is, people just didn't know what to say.

My husband also has an incredible visual memory, a trait that may contribute to the trauma he faces. He'll often share a memory or story, and he can provide distinct visual descriptions that I would never have noticed myself. This trait has kept him up at night, providing haunting memories of a pre–9/11 New York City.

"I still have dreams about the towers where I find myself walking through the buildings. I remember every detail of those buildings, down to how squishy the carpet was in the main lobby. These worries and dreams have faded over the years, but they're always in the back of my mind."

I'd love to tell you that other 9/11 Surviving Children had better experiences post–9/11, but it would be a lie. Jon's traumatic experiences are just the tip of the iceberg as we uncover what other 9/11 Surviving Children have to say.

MATTHEW BOCCHI

On September 18, what Matthew Bocchi's family feared most came true. Police officers arrived at the house to tell them that they'd found and identified his dad. At that time, they'd only been able to recover the lower half of his body, not finding the other portion until days later. Matthew was determined to learn about what happened to his father. Since they spoke with Matthew's dad on 9/11, he would ask his mom and father's brother repeatedly what he sounded like during phone calls. Soon, the obsession turned dark as Matthew turned to the internet for more information.

"I would spend hours in my room, in the dark, searching the internet, analyzing pictures of jumpers and recovered body parts from 9/11," Matthew writes in his book *Sway*.

In his book, he vulnerably shares how his manipulative Uncle Phil took advantage of this situation. Uncle Phil would encourage Matthew to talk about 9/11, feeding his obsession with what happened to his dad. Soon, the conversations changed, as Uncle Phil used Matthew's vulnerability to sexually abuse him. To numb the pain of the abuse and loss, Matthew turned to drugs to cope. Smoking pot by the age of sixteen, the drug use seemed harmless at first. It wasn't until his freshman year of college at Villanova that the problem became more evident. Soon, Matthew was buying and selling drugs; his favorites were Adderall, oxycodone, and cocaine, to name a few.

"I felt warm and fuzzy, the complete opposite of what I felt when thinking about my dad."

It wasn't long until Matthew turned around to find the drug use to be completely debilitating, ruining most of his relationships, job opportunities, and overall quality of life.

THEA TRINIDAD BUDGEN

Thea Trinidad found herself skipping school and going through the throws of depression by the time she was thirteen years old. She remembers the time being especially difficult for her and her brother.

"I didn't want to show emotion at all," Thea shares. She and her brother had to go to therapy, and Thea struggled with opening up or talking about anything. Instead, they found themselves lashing out in unpredictable ways. "We were mad at the world," she shares in a documentary with other 9/11 Surviving Children (The Children of 9/11 2019).

Like many other 9/11 Surviving Children, Thea found it difficult to communicate about her challenges, and avoiding therapy only exacerbated the issues. She seemed to be as unruly as her tousled, curly hair. Thea seemed to be missing a purpose or drive to keep her moving forward. Because Thea was unwilling to unravel her thoughts and feelings by talking about them in therapy or elsewhere, her emotions manifested into damaging behaviors.

For Thea, this turned into an eating disorder that would haunt her for years. In light of her father's death, Thea didn't feel that she deserved to be alive. She would do anything to bring her dad back in her place, so she looked for any opportunity for her to escape her reality. The fiery ball of energy that Thea was became a shell of herself, often contemplating cutting herself as a way to deal with her pain (Murphy 2021).

Purging food and inducing self-harm gave Thea a sense of control over her circumstances. Without healthy ways to handle her grief, she was struggling to find reasons to live.

While I didn't get to speak with Thea myself, I can see the pain in her eyes when watching her retell these dark memories in her interviews. Did she know how loved she was? Did she know that there are others like her who were going through the same thing? I wish I could go back in time and tell this hurting young girl who she would become: a world-renowned WWE wrestler.

THE THOMAS SISTERS

For Mary, Bridget, and Rose Thomas, the pain manifested into concerning behavior—very similar to what Thea had experienced.

To help process their emotions, Mary, Bridget, and Rose were all in therapy—and continue to be to this day. Both Mary and Bridget have struggled with eating disorders that they believe are directly tied to the loss of their dad.

Bridget would often use her eating disorder as psychological warfare against her mom, Ann. When the two found themselves in a fight, Bridget would intentionally say "I'm not going to eat," to make Ann angry. Always hurt by such a response, Ann would ask Bridget what she thinks her dad would say about this.

"I know that he'd be pissed," is what Bridget shared with me, but it wasn't enough to pull her away from these toxic behaviors. It's a battle that Bridget still struggles with to this day.

Their youngest sister, Rose, experienced anger and emotions that were difficult to control. As little as Rose was at the time of 9/11, processing the emotions of losing a parent you barely remember weighed on her. Even as Rose grew and learned how to speak, she used physical means to communicate how she was feeling. She would find herself lashing out at her mom and sisters, slamming doors behind her as she ran to her room to be alone.

Rose found her room as the only refuge she had and would spend many moments there cooling off from her anger or spending a sentimental moment thinking of her dad.

"I know I would always be in my bed and my mom would come knocking on my door and ask if I'm okay. I would tell her to leave me alone."

There was a coldness in Rose's voice as she recalled these moments. Rose and I spoke over the phone and the icy chill could still be felt through the line. It was as if she had been transported back to that lonely, dark place. It can be painful for me to handle moments like that. I'm quick to brush off pain and share a funny or happy anecdote to eliminate any and all discomfort. In this moment, however, I felt a call to sit in the pain with Rose. While staying there forever won't do either of us any good, lingering for just a minute longer allows us to fully feel and be with our emotions. It's when we recognize them that we can rise from them.

THE BURNETT SISTERS

Anna Clare, Halley, and Madison Burnett recall similar challenges when it came to dealing with their pain and the emotions that came along with it.

In the documentary *Children of 9/11*, Anna Clare shares how she would wake up screaming in the middle of the night (The Children of 9/11 2019). The actual nightmare they were living continued to haunt her in her dreams, and not even sleep allowed her to escape their reality.

Halley finds that death is now something she fears will visit her family prematurely again. Worry fills Halley's mind as she imagines all of the ways her mom might get sick or hurt and leave them. When violent tragedy like the one the Burnett's experienced comes to visit, it's hard to believe that something like that won't happen again. Irrational or not, the feeling can be difficult for Halley to shake, and she finds it impacts future decisions such as marriage and children.

"I'm not even dating anyone right now and yet I think about the life insurance plan I will someday need to get and the things I should do to make sure my family is taken care of if I were to suddenly die."

This realization and maybe even obsession with mortality is not uncommon amongst 9/11 Surviving Children. When exhibited in a healthy way, it can make a person more grateful for all the moments they do have with their loved ones. Unfortunately, it can also manifest into less attractive behaviors such as over-attachment to others. It's easy to see with experiences like these how one might get wrapped up in the fear of losing everyone around them.

As Halley shared her heart with me about the fear of losing her mother next, there was an aching in me that just wanted to remove this anxiety for her. If only there were a way to shield others from these types of things, but we know that is not the reality. I think about how her mom must feel, knowing that all efforts to protect her children from pain couldn't keep their father alive. When you hear how this trauma has impacted their lives, it's impossible to feel anything but immense empathy.

ALEXA EDWARDS

Once Alexa Edwards began engaging with peers at her school, it became painstakingly obvious that fitting in would prove to be difficult. As a small and timid child, Alexa would stand at the front of her school, knees shaking. Her principal would make his way down the hall and attempt to drag her to class. This was a daily occurrence that only seemed to worsen with time. The classroom setting was a difficult one for Alexa to adapt to, as the activities were often geared towards families with a mom and a dad. While the rest of the class doodled on their Father's Day cards, Alexa fidgeted uncomfortably, wishing that the end of the school day would come sooner.

Even while she learned to adapt to a school environment, getting and maintaining friendships proved difficult. Since most—if not all—of her peers had not lost a parent, Alexa felt afraid to share her pain with her friends.

It wasn't until a friend tragically lost her dad that she saw how others in similar situations deal with their grief. Her friend's journey showed her that while having those who "get it" around you can be helpful, that won't always be an option. Alexa began to realize that she might not connect with every single friend on all levels, and that's okay. Appreciating that all of these experiences are difficult, even if they look different than hers, was the key to greater empathy in her relationships.

Coming to this realization during her youth has greatly benefited Alexa's emotional intelligence as she continues to navigate life's challenges. It may even be true that losing her parent at a young age better prepared her to have greater emotional intelligence into her adulthood.

Through her relationships with friends, family, and her therapist, Alexa chose to step into her feelings about her grief. Whether that be through talking it out or sitting in her sadness for a time, Alexa can now revert back to these lessons every time she experiences challenges.

MARIA GARCIA

As an adult, Maria Garcia is strikingly aware of how 9/11 has impacted her mental health. As a child, she was less open to accepting how these events had an effect on her well-being. It is not surprising that Maria struggled to understand what she was feeling and why. Even still, her concerning reaction and behavior led to a diagnosis she carries with her to this day.

"I was diagnosed with posttraumatic stress disorder in relation to the events, which explains why certain memories of that time are fuzzy for me."

The images, videos, and sound effects that came out of 9/11 have been extremely triggering for Maria. It wasn't until Maria tried to watch a movie with violence in it that she recognized how this trauma continues to impact her. What seemed like a harmless experience left her with haunting nightmares. Most people wouldn't think twice about heading to the movie theater to watch a film; Maria finds that she has to be extremely thoughtful about her film choice.

Even growing up in New York, Maria found the empathy of her peers and elders to wear thin. Over the years, they seemed less and less aware that there are people who were directly impacted by these events.

Maria was seated in a middle-school classroom when she found herself distracted. Right next to her on the wall was a newspaper board with a clipping of the twin towers on 9/11. Maria couldn't keep her eyes off of that board, leaving her anxious and unable to learn. But when she mentioned her situation to the teacher and asked for a seat change, Maria found her teacher to be less than sympathetic.

"The teacher was not very supportive, and told me to just get over it."

Unfortunately, Maria's struggle to distance herself from her triggers continued. Another teacher, who was a first responder on 9/11, shared a graphic retelling of his experience on the anniversary of the day. Maria sat in the room for as long as she could before removing herself from the situation.

"I just bolted. I was always a runner. That was how I dealt with my feelings."

Even with the resources of therapy to guide her, Maria was resistant to treatment and used physical means to lash out. Running away from her problems seemed like the best way out, even when it presented more challenges for her.

Even still, Maria had a strong parental figure who showed her proper responses to her challenges. Self-preservation, for one, is a learned trait that Maria inherited from her mother. Maria Garcia's mom needed to set boundaries for what she was open to learning about the fate of her husband.

"It was Easter of 2002, and we came home to find the police outside of our house. They told us they had found some of his remains. My mom kindly asked them to respectfully not notify her of any future remains found."

This took an immense amount of strength for Maria's mom to decide, and this resilience is something that sticks with Maria to this day.

"My mom is a badass and I am who I am today because of her." Maria's face lit up when she mentioned her mom's name. The "can-do" attitude that her mom has is a trait that Maria looks to when walking through her own challenges.

MARK LYNCH

Because Mark was a baby at the time of 9/11, it was always a part of Mark's reality that his dad wasn't alive. By the time Mark was in kindergarten, he realized that his family looked a bit different than his friends'.

Even today, the mentioning of "parents" or "dad" in social or educational settings makes him sweat. The feeling that others might be looking at him and realizing his family makeup looks different, even if they don't know his situation, still haunts him to this day.

Mark wouldn't experience the pain of death again until his dog died in second grade. For many children, the death of a pet is the first time they come to terms with this inevitable part of life. For Mark, it was a reminder of what he had already lost. "Why does this always happen to me!" Mark exclaimed.

Resisting a chuckle as Mark told me this story was hard. Even he looks back on this time and now laughs at this sentiment. But for second-grade Mark, this connection to the loss of his father was very real and painful.

CAT BRENNAN

Cat Brennan finds herself in a similar predicament to Mark. She grew up in a time where 9/11 was being taught and talked about in school. Cat found that it was best to let teachers know in advance of her situation.

Cat began every school year with a candid chat with her teachers. She would start each year with, "Hey, so I lost my dad in 9/11 and I'm open to learning about it, but I would appreciate you letting me know the content you're going to share ahead of time so I can decide whether I want to participate or not."

I cannot even fathom having to do this. These are difficult things to have to learn at any age, and yet the 9/11 Surviving Children were forced to do so when they were very young. Learning self-preservation and advocacy early on became a central key to their success in later years.

PETE DAVIDSON

Pete Davidson has opened up in some of his early Comedy Central shows that he "was lucky it happened when [he] was seven," because at that age, "you don't understand things." Even though he was young, Pete still found himself in and out of therapy since he was nine years old. He even shared that he once tried to drown himself in a pool (Roberts 2020).

Pete was in therapy soon after 9/11—an experience he still jokes about today.

"My therapist was Afghan. He would be like, 'How do you think your dad died?' I always wanted to be like, 'Why don't you tell me, man? I know you know.'" (Juzwiak 2018).

Even Pete himself recognizes this joke is a bit dark. He shares that when this joke is told in a set, "Five people will laugh, and the rest will be like, 'Hmmmm, no.' But it's f***n' funny!" (Juzwiak 2018).

Making a joke out of his loss seems to be the best way that Pete knows how to handle his life experiences. "Things that I feel really sad about, I talk about. That way, if it's funny, it doesn't hurt anymore." (Juzwiak 2018).

Pete's trials didn't end with the loss of his father. He was diagnosed with Crohn's disease, an inflammatory bowel disease that can cause abdominal pain and other digestive tract issues. Those who suffer from Crohn's disease sometimes also experience rings around their eyes—something that is distinctive about Pete Davidson's look. Given his popularity and time in the public eye, many have negatively commented on his gaunt look and used his personal challenges with drugs and depression in an effort to sell articles.

Crohn's can be a debilitating disease, oftentimes taking those who suffer from it away from doing what they love. Coupling that with the trauma of losing his father would make it seem like Pete would never be able to become the incredible comedian he is today. Even with his perseverance to make his dream happen, Pete has continued to battle drug abuse issues that have led him to continue his therapy and take antidepressants to ease the pain (Juzwiak 2018).

But not all is lost for Pete, who found community amongst firefighter families who knew and loved his dad. His closeness with them even led to the featuring of many real firefighters in his 2020 film, *The King of Staten Island.*

Even with his sick and twisted sense of humor, his chronic illness, and drug abuse, this comedy giant (literally, Pete is six foot three!) does have a sentimental bone in his body, fondly remembering his father on social media on every anniversary of 9/11. It's in these moments where I think we get a true glimpse into who Pete really is. The jokes, while hilarious at times, have a way of masking the person within.

REBECCA ASARO

Like Pete Davidson, Rebecca Asaro found camaraderie within the firefighting community after her dad died. Rebecca recalls the Chief visiting to check in on her family and continuing that relationship for years to come. They also had the support of counselors, who began making regular visits to the home.

Rebecca remembers being resistant to therapy as a kid but recognized how important it was by the time she was in her twenties.

"Things became really tough for me around the time of the memorial opening at Ground Zero. I would hear a song that reminded me of my dad and I would just fall apart. I would have dreams of my dad and of the towers collapsing. I had anxiety and would panic every time I heard a plane overhead. I finally went back to talk to someone and realized how much of these challenges were tied to my past."

Many of the 9/11 Surviving Children's challenges are steeped in the reality that many of them never recovered their parent's remains. Rebecca has said that not ever finding her dad made it hard for her family to find closure, but that she's not sure how identifying him now would change things.

"You go from seeing someone every day to them up and leaving with no real explanation or body. And I hear stories all the time of how they are still identifying people and I just don't know if I want to reopen that wound. I've gotten used to the mindset I'm currently in and am okay with closing that chapter."

It's almost as if receiving a call today that her dad's remains had been found would drudge up a piece of her heart she's already closed off. There's a certain amount of strength that comes with self-preservation. It's a strength I have come to understand all too well with my own challenges.

NICOLE FOSTER

Like many others, Nicole Foster's family has never identified any remains of her father. The experience of trying to identify remains has been a traumatic one for her family. The journey began with investigators asking for her dad's dental records. This painful experience seemed to lie dormant in Nicole's mind until May of 2014, when the 9/11 Memorial Museum opened to the public. The museum is an extension of the 9/11 memorial which now stands in the original place of the Twin Towers. Nicole and her family, along with other 9/11 families, were invited to visit the museum before the public.

"Inside the museum is a giant wall and behind it is a room where the remains are. It's just a bunch of cabinets and things that you wouldn't imagine are people's remains at all. The whole thing was very bizarre, and it was the first time I felt anything close to a cemetery for my dad and there it was on display. I think that's why there's never been a place that feels like a proper resting place".

Unfortunately, Nicole's challenges didn't stop after 9/11. Nicole's older sister is special needs, which presented a greater challenge to her mom who now led life as a single parent. To make matters more difficult, just before her fifteenth birthday, Nicole was diagnosed with Acute promyelocytic leukemia (APML).

"The experience reminded me that I had already survived so much already, and I really had faith that I would survive again, even though I was scared. I just told myself, 'I'm going to get through this' and that's what I did."

While her doctor's assured her that the leukemia was very treatable, a cancer diagnosis doesn't tend to be on the birthday wish list for any fifteen-year-old. Nicole attributes an additional diagnoses of generalized anxiety disorder with her cancer diagnoses and the loss of her father. Luckily for Nicole, she has been able to get help for her anxiety through counselors and medication.

There is a boldness in the way Nicole speaks about taking the time and care to get the treatment she needed for recovery. Her freedom and vulnerability paved the way for my own as I continue to share my challenges with others.

ANNE NELSON

Anne Nelson and her family's worries about her dad were confirmed two weeks after 9/11.

"I remember police officers in unmarked vehicles and a priest from our church pulling up to the house. I was outside skateboarding with some friends, and I just had this strange feeling that came over me when I saw them all pull up. I knew something serious was going on. I walked inside and there were ten people huddled in our small living room. They had informed my mom that they had found my father. I feel thankful that we were one of the few families who actually got to have their loved ones remains recovered."

For Anne, there is a pride that comes along with the discovery of her dad's remains. A few days before he was identified, Anne and her sister had gone to a hotel near the Newark airport in New Jersey where the Red Cross swabbed their mouths. The DNA collected that day was used to help locate their father.

"I was proud to be able to be a part of that process of bringing him to rest."

Even with the pride that came with that moment, Anne recognizes how painful these days were. She recalls just going through the motions, doing what needed to be done during that time, and later reflecting on the immensity of the situation. Like many other 9/11 Surviving Children, Anne attended therapy sessions, something that would become even more important to her after tragedy struck their family again.

In April of 2017, Anne's sister Caitlin died unexpectedly at the age of twenty. Caitlin was trying to raise money for charity with her sorority in college when she started aspirating. She was placed on a ventilator for a few days before she died in the hospital.

"I think that loss is what really made me process my father's death a little more. Even though I had gone to therapy before, the enormity of it all didn't really hit me until that happened."

Anne mentions how there were parts of her that were lost after 9/11.

"After I lost my father, I experienced challenges with anxiety. Prior to 9/11, I was carefree and courageous. I feel that 9/11 erased some of those qualities, or at least put them aside. Because my father used to coach my sports teams, after 9/11, my perspective was that playing sports wouldn't be the same without him as my coach. So, I stopped playing sports—even though I enjoyed them—and instead became overly obsessed with my academic performance."

I couldn't help but feel immense sadness for Anne as she shared this. I could feel the burden she put on this younger version of herself like a heavy weight. Even for me, breathing under the enormity of this pressure was hard. I could only hope that the rest of Anne's story would find her tossing this weight from her life for good!

WHAT RULES YOUR LIFE?

Many of the 9/11 Surviving Children shared with me that recalling even the most traumatic moments of their lives has been therapeutic for them. It's never easy uncovering these difficult moments, but they know something we can't yet see: the rest of their stories get *better*. That's the funny thing about hitting "rock bottom". The only way you can go is up.

So how do we possibly find the light when it's too dark to see? And how do we make sense of these tragic events? Recalling the study I shared earlier from Tominey, O'Byron, Rivers, and Shapses, the secret lies in how 9/11 Surviving Children's childhood trauma fostered emotional intelligence.

Drawing from Mayer and Salovey's (1997) refined theory of emotional intelligence, Brackett and Rivers (2014) identified five skills that can be taught to increase emotional intelligence: recognizing emotions in oneself and others; understanding the causes and consequences of emotions; labeling emotions accurately; expressing emotions in ways that are appropriate for the time, place, and culture; and regulating emotions. These skills, which form the acronym RULER, are the heart of an effective approach for modeling emotional intelligence and teaching the emotional intelligence skills children need to be ready to learn (Tominey, O'Byron, Rivers, and Shapses 2017).

These interviews are living proof that many 9/11 Surviving Children have been likely using RULER without even knowing it. If this is true, one can infer that others who have experienced trauma have used or can use elements of RULER too. By implementing RULER, we can help to ensure that our emotions do not rule our lives.

MY OWN TRAUMA

———

Speaking with 9/11 Surviving Children made me think about how skills like RULER and otherwise might be playing out in my own life. When I reflect on my own experience with my emotions, I find that I am quick to make judgements about how I'm feeling rather than taking the first two steps of recognizing these emotions and understanding their causes. I get stuck in what I call my "positivity box."

Being upbeat and positive is a trait I've often prided myself in. Even when I share some of the most painful moments of my life with others, I do so with a smile on my face. This can often lead to the perception that I'm not actually sad and that things are okay. With sentiments like "You're always so positive!" I don't feel I have permission to be anything else. The feelings are bad, which means I am bad. Could it be that the feelings are just feelings? That they are neither bad nor good; they are just responses and not a direct reflection of my "goodness"?

I've started taking one breath. Then two breaths. I take a moment to analyze rather than judge what I am feeling. Some key questions I ask are: How does it make my body feel? What might have triggered this behavior or reaction?

The more I have taken the time to acknowledge how I'm feeling and understand what may be causing it, the better I've found that I can regulate my emotions. This is a big difference from trying to *control* my emotions, which, like most attempts to control things, often fails.

Instead, I find ways to avoid triggers where I can. I hide social media posts of pregnancy announcements. By limiting my feed, I limit what social media junk I'm willing to feed myself. In the same way I choose who has access to my story, the same is true for who and what I let in.

Like the defensive line of a football team (a good one, I think!), I protect my heart. And yet, life still throws things our way that we can't avoid. I can't hide from every pregnancy announcement, especially when so many of my friends are having success in growing their families. I won't be able to avoid every hurtful comment. Let's face it: there have even been interviews for this book where reporters have asked if I have kids yet!

For the times when I can't just run away and hide, I call on the offensive line to come out and play. This is the place where skills like RULER live.

So, I take one breath. Then two breaths. I put on my helmet to protect my mind and the shoulder pads to guard my heart. I remember the lessons of RULER, and for a moment, I've made the touchdown.

BADASS

While there are certainly times where I do feel like a badass, I can assure you it's not in the doctor's office. As my fertility journey has had me in and out of doctor's offices for two years, I haven't gotten any better at advocating for myself. And when I do, it tends to go horribly wrong.

Right before I started Letrozole—a fertility drug that can help trigger a "superovulation" (yes, that does mean a chance for multiples!)—the visit before, my doctor had asked me to fill out a calendar, writing down the days in which I was sexually active and my basal body temperature for each day. The overachiever in me took it up a notch, color-coding the whole thing. I wasn't new to this type of tracking; I had been doing it myself with the help of apps and other tools for quite some time. The biggest difference is that the doctor wanted me to keep tracking up until day one of the next cycle.

For women who are trying to get pregnant, the two weeks prior to the next cycle (often called the two-week wait) can be extremely stressful. At that point in your cycle, there is literally nothing left to do but wait, either for cycle day one to come or a positive pregnancy test. I found that keeping this detailed calendar and temp checking on these days added to my anxiety. I had a plan to walk into the office and ask if it would be alright if I stopped tracking after I've confirmed ovulation to help ease my nerves. The doctor said no, and the student doctor in the room asked me why tracking during those two weeks gave me anxiety.

At that moment the badass in me left the building, and the tears started to flow.

If I couldn't trust my doctors—the people who must work with countless women on their fertility journeys—to be sympathetic, who could I trust?

I also find that when my doctor gives me a new piece of information, I'm not good at asking for what I need up front. I typically need time to collect my thoughts and develop my response. This was true when my doctor told me that he had eight refills of Letrozole available for me at my pharmacy, which meant that if I didn't get pregnant before that,

I could be on this drug for eight months. When we'd already been trying for so long, that seemed like a very long time, especially when I had seen research that the effectiveness of this drug typically wears off after three months. Instead of speaking up for what I needed, I left feeling deflated.

Cat is a badass for telling her teacher what she needs. Maria's mom is a badass for advocating for boundaries for herself. The 9/11 Surviving Families are full of badasses. I want to be one, too.

My doctor isn't a mind reader, and at the end of the day, I am consulting him for an opinion and am in charge of what I do with my own body. That next month, I decided to not take any of the fertility drugs or do any of the tracking, and I have never felt freer. For my next appointment with my doctor, I came with a written list of the things I wanted to cover. This left little room for me to leave without getting the answers I needed.

What I learned from the 9/11 Surviving Children is that a little preparedness goes a long way. Before a tough conversation, I've started writing down what I need to say in advance. This ensures that I don't leave before I say what I needed to say. It's my little form of badassery. It might not seem like much, but to me it is everything.

BLACK CLOTHS

As I spoke with the 9/11 Surviving Children about their traumatic experiences with the 9/11 Memorial Museum and recovery of their loved ones, I could immediately connect with their trepidation.

My husband and I have yet to visit the museum portion of the memorial. His stepmom and one of his brothers had the opportunity to visit themselves. They shared with Jon that it is a thoughtfully curated museum and an extremely emotional experience, especially for those who were personally affected by this tragedy. Jon has decided that he isn't ready for this experience and may never be.

My whole 9/11 experience has me sitting somewhere in the middle. Like a tightrope walker, I like to see myself as delicately balancing between proud American citizen who honors 9/11 with a "Never Forget" post each year, and wife in the thick of how this day impacted my husband's life, and now my own. Truth is, I often feel like I'm stumbling on the wire more times than I'm balanced.

With almost three thousand people dying in 9/11, the remains of more than one thousand of them remain unidentified to this day. The human remains, which are made up of skeletal fragments and tissue, are mostly so small that they are about the size of "a Tic Tac," as described by one medical examiner (Idov 2011). On May 10, 2014, just days before the 9/11 Memorial Museum was to open, 7,930 of these remains were transferred to their final resting place within the museum. The examiners continue to study and identify those remains, making the museum part laboratory as well.

Many 9/11 Surviving Families struggle with this display at the museum. The police and fire department cavalcade that escorted the remains that day was met with protestors wearing black cloths over their mouths. Many felt that the remains should be a part of the memorial rather than the museum, where they would be placed underground in a manner that many deemed disrespectful (Pengelly 2014).

One protester, who lost her firefighter son, told the Associated Press: "I don't know how much of him is down here. If it's one little inch, I want it treated respectfully. I want it above ground. I don't want it to be part of a museum. I don't want it to be part of a freak show." (Pengelly 2014).

The thing is, I *want* to go to the museum. And no, it's not a part of some trauma-porn obsession. As an American, I want to learn more about that part of our history. As a wife of a 9/11 Surviving Child, I want to connect with my husband without him having to be the one to tell me about it. No doubt it will be a challenging visit for me, as I try to imagine my husband at thirteen years old living through this tragedy. But I will know this part of him more deeply and intimately than I could ever ask him to share with me himself.

In a most unfortunate parallel, it's likely that during my next visit to the memorial and museum, I will also be wearing a black cloth—not necessarily in protest, but in true pandemic fashion. Even still, I will hold the protestors and all those who feel conflicted about the museum in my heart as I try to understand the complex decisions that went into creating a museum of such magnitude.

I see the opportunity to visit the memorial as an opportunity to connect with my husband. It's likely that he lived firsthand the very devastating things that are in this museum, which is why visiting could be so triggering for him. But the same is true every time I ask him painful questions about 9/11. Jon has been open and honest about his story which I am forever grateful for. It does make me wonder if at some point, others' desire to connect with him could cause him pain. While Jon usually doesn't protest when asked to share his experiences, I can only imagine that the drudging up of these memories can be detrimental to his health.

I had an amazing conversation with Kathleen Thomas (K), an Associate Professional Clinical Counselor at North County Lifeline, who explained to me exactly how this works.

K has a breadth of experience in this topic as she works to support and provide guidance to victims of human trafficking.

She shared that for many people with posttraumatic stress disorder or who experience traumatic events, every time they share their story, it often can retrigger and retraumatize them. My heart broke. How many times have these 9/11 Surviving Children been asked to share their stories? Am I a part of the problem by asking them to share again?

Even for myself, there are days where I struggle to muster up the courage to have these interviews or write these words down on the page. I recognize this, and yet I can't help but want to learn more.

COUNTING

There have been plenty of infuriating things that people have said to me during our fertility journey. My favorite has to be, "You need to relax. Don't stress. Just calm down and get pregnant." Nothing makes my head want to spin off its axis more than this comment. If they only knew the great lengths I go through to keep my mind off all of the stressors that life and infertility have brought us.

To be fair, I've got a few balls in my court at the moment. I'll often hear from others that they just don't know how I do it all: write a book; work full time; cope with Jon's unemployment for over a year, and start fertility treatments. The thing is, no one can do it all. I certainly can't. And in an effort to try to do so, it's usually my mental health that takes a backseat to accommodate the other commitments.

There have been several days that have been challenging, but one stands out in particular. That morning started out just like any other day. I let our two dogs out into our fenced backyard and headed to my cozy spot to start writing. About ten minutes in, I notice I couldn't hear my Yorkie outside. He typically is crying to come in after being out for three seconds. He is our resident drama king. My husband opens the sliding door to find our Pomeranian, bright-eyed and bushy-tailed, staring back at us. Our Yorkie, nowhere to be found. I bolt out the front door, screaming my dog's name: "Rex! Rex, *where* are you?"

In my mind, I was screaming too. "Why is this happening to me? Will I *ever* get a break?"

That day was "Florida cold" (in the forties), and I remember shivering, the tears freezing on my face as I ran up and down the streets of our neighborhood. Jon had gotten into his car to start looking for him that way. We had been searching for over thirty minutes. I had already posted on our Facebook and Nextdoor neighborhood groups when we found him, soaking wet and shaking.

We couldn't have been happier when he was returned to us, and I was hoping this meant our day would turn around. Then our heat broke, bringing temps in the fifties into our house. To top it all off, I had a pretty terrible work meeting that upended a high-visibility project I was working on at the time.

I felt sick, stressed, and angry with not only my circumstances but the way I had responded to them. I immediately thought of my husband, cool as a cucumber and doing a much better job of managing everything that fell on our plate that day.

Even with that thought of "What would Jon do?" I recognized that it hadn't always been this way for him. Even with years of practice, there are still times where the stressors of his childhood bubble up and impact his response to certain situations. A common reaction for Jon on days like that one is to avoid the pain of it at all costs. This often includes taking a nap, which has to be the most infuriating response for me—someone who wants to take action to fix everything.

And yet, how can I possibly blame him for this type of reaction? How can I shame any of the 9/11 Surviving Children who acted out or coped in unhealthy ways after their lives were upended?

Children acting out or experiencing challenges posttrauma is not uncommon. In fact, when I began my research, I thought that would be the most resounding and long-lasting impact on the children of 9/11. According to the National Child Traumatic Stress Network (NCTSN), children who have experienced complex trauma often have difficulty identifying, expressing, and managing emotions; and may have limited language for feeling states. They often internalize and/or externalize stress reactions and, as a result, may experience significant depression, anxiety, or anger. (Peterson 2018).

I was having difficulty expressing my emotions in healthy ways myself, and I don't even have a childhood trauma to blame for it! From this research, I could quickly understand why the most traumatic years of many 9/11 Surviving Children were rife with frustration. I dug a bit deeper to understand how this trauma sticks with those who experience it throughout their lives.

According to the Centers for Disease Control and Prevention (CDC), "When children develop long term symptoms (longer than one month) from such stress, which are upsetting or interfere with their relationships and activities, they may be diagnosed with posttraumatic stress disorder (PTSD). Even mildly stressful situations or reminders of the traumatic event can have varying effects on a child's mood and behavior. Since the biology of a child is defined by both nature and nurture in their development stages, these behaviors and responses can lead to life-long behavioral patterns. (Centers for Disease Control and Prevention 2021).

When the 9/11 Surviving Children mentioned some of their many physical responses to their emotional problems (running away, lashing out in anger, etc.), I thought of my own physical responses to grief and even stress. That tension I carry in my shoulders. The clenched jaw and fists. The upset stomach. I thought that the exterior pain must be connected to the interior.

K, my contact at North County Lifeline, was able to shed some light on this. She shared that our grief and trauma are actually tied to our nervous system, which is why we tend to react in physical ways. In fact, many of the triggers we encounter are oftentimes physical in nature as well.

"Imagine you were walking down the street and you are assaulted by someone wearing Calvin Klein cologne. You're in the grocery store a week later, and you smell that same cologne again. Your body tenses up, because you now associate that smell with danger. This is built into our systems to protect us and is normal, but can be detrimental when it continues past thirty days or so."

I worried that this innate, animalistic response we have when our bodies sense danger means we are unhealable. I was ready to wash my hands of the whole thing and consider myself a lost cause. I felt that I would forever be trapped in my body, a victim to my nervous system and its responses.

Then I remembered something: first, I'm not a victim; second, I remembered one of the 9/11 Surviving Children, Rose, telling me that she would take a hot shower to calm herself down.

I wondered if it is possible that we can use physical things to combat our physical reactions?

K says yes. "You can try running your hands under cool water or hold an ice cube in your hand and take a moment to think about how that sensation feels. Take a sip of water and observe how that feels going down your throat. Sometimes even taking an inventory of the room, counting how many of an object are there, can distract you from your reaction and reground you."

I had an opportunity on that hectic, winter morning to change my story. I wanted to clench my fist. Clench my jaw. Tense my shoulders. I could feel the stomachache starting. Instead, I stopped. One breath. Two breaths. I looked around my office. I counted the light bulbs hanging from my string lights above my desk. I counted the Disney Tsum Tsums displayed on the shelf. I counted everything I could, until I felt the physical responses pass.

I'm glad I talked to K when I did, but I'm still envious of those who have already learned these skills and have been using them to support their growth for years. This doesn't mean I wanted the loss that came with it, but I did want to keep digging in more so that other people like myself can be freed from the impacts of PTSD.

This meant I would need to learn more about PTSD and how it impacts children who experience great loss, like the 9/11 Surviving Children. I had the opportunity to sit down with Stacie Boyar, a Licensed Mental Health Counselor in Coral Springs, Florida, who was able to share more about the phenomenon.

Boyar has had her fair share of working with children who have experienced trauma. On February 18, 2018, a gunman with a semiautomatic rifle walked into nearby Marjory

Stoneman Douglas High School and opened fire, killing seventeen people. Much of Boyar's work has been focused on healing the community of Parkland, Florida, which is still grieving from the event.

According to Boyar, "PTSD is a mental health condition that affects people who have experienced or witnessed or even heard about a traumatic event. This disorder can lead to increased anxiety, chronic fight-or-flight stress, harmful attachments to others, and self-medicating."

Turns out PTSD doesn't just happen for those who experience an event for themselves. Those who hear about it secondhand can also experience the effects of PTSD.

"I was seeing a young girl who began seeing the effects of PTSD after hearing a story from her friend's sister. They were hanging out in the house and the sister recalled her experiences and what she went through during the school shooting."

Just like secondhand smoke, the stories we hear can poison us, too. This realization made me defensive at first. *I don't have a problem with 9/11—I didn't lose anyone that day!* And yet, I've heard the story about Jon's dad so many times that I start to picture what it must have been like: Calling home. Telling your family you're safe. Then running back into the massive, burning building. I imagine the confusion my husband must have felt in those first few days. The desperation he felt when he realized his dad wasn't coming home. The regret from not being able to remember their last conversation. This weighs on all of me, too. Because I did lose someone that day: I lost my father-in-law. I lost the grandfather to my future children. I missed out on someone who I would most likely be seeking advice from, and spending time with, had he survived.

I feel the guilt that I have asked the 9/11 Surviving Children to relive these experiences for this project. I shared this with K, and she assured me that many who suffer from trauma are often able to find great purpose in sharing their challenges with others. When they rationalize that they are telling their stories to help others like them, it becomes easier for them to bear. I have felt this in my interviews and even heard it from some of the 9/11 Surviving Children I've spoken to. I've even experienced it for myself when I give myself another pep talk to get through the next interview.

I'm grateful for all of the 9/11 Surviving Children who opened their hearts to me for this purpose, but I still feel the immense pressure to make certain I do them justice.

Thinking of it all makes me want to clench my fist. Clench my jaw. Tense my shoulders. Somedays, I still do. But somedays, I count. And at least for a short time, I feel okay.

INNER CHILD

Jon and I started seeing a therapist about a year into our infertility journey. Whenever we show up to therapy thinking we have nothing to talk about is when all of the good healing happens. One particular conversation started with laughter and casual banter and quickly took a turn toward deeper conversation. It was few days after receiving word from our fertility specialist that our best option of conceiving was IUI or IVF (in vitro fertilization). At that point, we had made the decision to forgo both options (at least for the time being). Instead, we planned a one-month road trip in our Airstream to travel the country as safely as possible mid-pandemic.

As we were avid travelers pre-COVID (in fact, it pains me to think of all our canceled trips—RIP) this trip was more than exciting. We knew that this might be our only opportunity to do something like this while I was still working remotely and Jon remained jobless. We also recognized that if we were to move forward with fertility treatments we would have to stay put for a while, since IUI isn't something that can be performed via telehealth. Plus, this household loves a good distraction from our pain, and this trip was fitting the bill.

I thought we'd spend much of our session talking about the trip and our plans, but as soon as I mentioned how this meant putting our trying to conceive on hold, I broke down. I had prayed so specifically to be able to conceive naturally, and it was just hitting me right there that this likely wouldn't be possible. Again, I was grieving for the plans I had made, as well as my body's inability to do what it's designed to do. As someone who has often put her worth in her work, trying to get pregnant and failing every month feels like a great big "F" on the report card.

Our therapist asked if I knew that I am worthy and loved just by *being* me. I couldn't even rationalize that concept. I thought I knew better—that no one could possibly love me unless I was being successful. This thinking is a key reason as to why I've been suffering through this so much—I've associated my worth with getting pregnant.

Our therapist asked if there was anything I needed to tell my inner child that might help to heal the misconceptions I have around loving myself. She shared how each of us has an inner child and that it is quite literally the child that lives on within all of us. Her explanation was that it often makes a more outward appearance when triggered by something we experienced in our childhood. She believed that my disappointment and anger at myself was a direct reflection of expectations set for me as a child.

She handed over a list of phrases that I should share out loud with my inner child. "I love you, no matter what" and "You are worthy of love, care, and affection" are some of the few that stirred my spirit. I couldn't ever imagine saying these to myself.

After leaving me with that exercise, we turned over to Jon. I figured "Mr. Resilient" wouldn't have any affirmations that he struggled with. The therapist asked if there was anything on the list that resonated with Jon. I heard his quiet, ashamed voice say, "I'm proud of you."

My heart instantly broke. Why in the *world* is Jon not proud of himself? Have I not told him enough times how amazing he is? Turns out, it doesn't matter how many times you tell someone something unless they believe it themselves.

We started digging into this statement and traced it back to a memory from one of the 9/11 Surviving Children camps he had attended many years ago. He recalled an exercise where he wrote a letter to his dad, tied it to a small raft, and sent it floating away on a lake. In the letter, he told his dad that he would step in and take care of his brothers. In Jon's mind, he failed to do what he wrote in the years that followed. He feels that school and other activities got in the way of him being able to do what he promised. Because of this, he feels his dad, his family, and his brothers are not proud of him.

This statement could not be further from the truth. I've seen how his brothers adore him. All three of them were involved in theatre throughout their lives because they saw their big brother on the stage. His youngest brother, Mark, would most likely jump off a bridge if Jon had done it. Together they share many hobbies and interests, from camping to Disney.

Not one person expected a thirteen-year-old Jon to step in and try to be a father figure. Not one person, except Jon himself.

It took until this moment for me to understand that even with how resilient my husband is, he still has an inner child to deal with. We've both got work to do, but we'll get there— *together.* And someday, our inner children will run free and unashamed. They will love themselves unconditionally. After all, we are human *beings*, not human *doings*. We don't have to *do* anything at all to be loved.

THE SIGNS

—

From memories to memorabilia, many families have found comfort in the things that keep their loved one's memory alive. Beyond this, there seems to be something else at play giving 9/11 Surviving Children the sense of their parents' presence wherever they go.

Early on in the interview process, I assumed that many in this group would have experienced the feelings of wanting to do right by their parent. Jon has often shared that he feels his dad is watching over him, and that he tries to live in a way that would make him proud. What I didn't expect were the bone-chilling spiritual signs and experiences many of them would share with me. As I began to clearly see a pattern amongst my interviews, I became more intentional about asking questions about the signs that 9/11 Surviving Children believe they receive from their loved ones.

Whether you believe in signs from the other side or not, it's clear that these "visits" from family members often arrived at key times and gave hope, peace, and clarity to many of the 9/11 Surviving Children. Litsa Williams, a clinical social worker who has worked in the field for 12 years, believes it best to lean into these moments rather than discredit them.

She writes, "When you feel your loved one's presence, feel it without apology or any worry that you are crazy! This is a normal and helpful way we continue bonds with our loved ones." (Williams 2021)

For the purpose of the healing that these signs have brought to 9/11 Surviving Children, I ask the reader to put their skepticism aside and explore the moments that have helped so many in their road to recovery.

MATTHEW BOCCHI

For Matthew Bocchi and his mother, that sign came in the form of a fly that stayed in their house for six months after his dad, John, died.

"Each time a fly showed up in my life, a feeling of peace and tranquility swept over me," Matthew writes in his book *Sway*. "At that point, I began addressing the fly as Dad."

Matthew also mentions that the fly continues to show up at pivotal points in his life, whether it be big decisions or big events. It's as if the "fly on the wall" idiom has taken on a brand-new meaning for Matthew and his family. These moments with the fly have given Matthew peace that his dad approves and that things will work out for the best.

The most prominent moment came when Matthew was at rock bottom. In the midst of his addiction, he was in desperate need of rehabilitation. Grappling with the reality of his debilitated state, Matthew was searching for encouragement in his darkest hour. While standing on the porch steps of his home, he saw a fly that he immediately identified as his dad. At that moment, Matthew felt called to turn away from his demons and seek out the help he needed. While efforts to complete rehab programs and recover in the past had failed, something flipped inside Matthew's mind after this experience. It was as if his moment with the fly was the push he needed to make a serious change.

THE THOMAS SISTERS

For Mary, Bridget, and Rose Thomas, their belief is that their dad comes to them in a form of a ladybug. Both Ann and Rose share fond memories of ladybugs making appearances in their lives.

Their mom, Ann, recalls several instances in the dead of winter where lady bugs have shown up:

"Ladybugs are our thing. It was one day in January and I was feeling as gloomy as the weather outside. And with that, in the middle of winter, across my kitchen counter crawled a ladybug. Then that February, we went to Pennsylvania to stay at my Aunt's timeshare. My cousin's kids were calling me from different rooms because there were seven ladybugs throughout the timeshare."

For Rose, ladybugs don't make her sad about missing her dad, but rather uplift her with a feeling that her dad is communicating with her.

"Whenever a ladybug lands on us we think it's our dad," Rose shared with a smile in her voice. It was the most joyful moment of my interview with Rose. I got the sense that for Rose, who cannot remember her father, these moments where her dad pops in to say "Hello" provide more connection with him than any item of his ever could.

MARK LYNCH

The Thomas family isn't the only one that believes that ladybugs are a visit from their lost parent. Ladybugs have been a sign for Mark Lynch and his family as well. Mark never thought much of it until he purchased his first camper. Since

Mark is my brother-in-law, I was able to get one of the first looks at his proud new purchase. I remember the moment I first stepped foot inside the camper. More accurately, I should say my foot went *through* the camper. The floor had all but rotted out, bowing in the middle under our weight. A musty smell permeated the entire camper, likely a result of the water damage and dated upholstery.

Jon and I kept a brave face in front of Mark, encouraging him that with a little love, this camper had a lot of potential. I shared my less optimistic concerns with Jon after being out of earshot from Mark.

Even Mark acknowledges that the camper was a bit rough around the edges and mentions having buyer's remorse right after the purchase. That was until he noticed ladybug wings scattered throughout the camper. A calm suddenly came over him at the sight.

"At first it was kind of disgusting, but then I felt good about it seeing that sign. It solidified the purchase for me as a good one."

Jon remained optimistic as well, and soon the two had planned a remodel of the entire camper. Mark made the drive from New Jersey to Florida and they spent a month renovating the entire space. They ripped out and replaced the whole floor before they repainted and replaced the upholstery. Even though I knew that the two of them could do anything they put their minds to, I was still astonished by the incredible work that they were able to accomplish together. It was a process of labor and love that I know their dad, a handyman himself, would be proud of.

As we neared the end of the project, we FaceTimed in Mark and Jon's family so they could see the project. Mid-FaceTime call, I noticed a living ladybug right next to the window. I jumped out of my seat and immediately shared with everyone. We all agreed it was a sign from their dad.

JON LYNCH

When I began digging deeper into these signs, I immediately knew what Jon would say. Seeing the numbers "911" have become such a common occurrence for Jon that it's almost as second nature as breathing.

"I see 9:11 on the clock all the time and I just say 'Hey Dad' every time. He is here with me, and I'm always grateful when he lets me know he's there."

My favorite part of this is how casual of a recognition this is for Jon. We could be cooking breakfast in the morning or getting ready for bed in the evening when 9:11 rolls around on the clock. The gentle smile that Jon shares is all the proof I need that he is at peace with these signs.

Jon is not alone in this experience. It was something that almost every 9/11 Surviving Child I spoke with mentioned. These were some of my favorite moments during the interviews, where I could exclaim, "Us, too!" about a positive experience rather than a negative one.

CAT BRENNAN

For Cat Brennan, who wasn't old enough to know her dad before her family lost him, seeing signs that he is with her can be challenging.

"I often joke that my dad is trying to tell me something really great and I just don't know what it is!"

Without having known her dad personally, Cat feels that she struggles to recognize signs from her dad in the way her mom does. And yet, Cat's mom says that Cat's personality alone is all the proof she needs that her dad is there with them. It is her belief that the outgoing nature that Cat and her dad share are a friendly way of him saying "Hello."

Cat appreciates the sentiment but struggles to make the connection herself. Instead, she looks forward to a few fleeting moments where she feels his presence.

"I was taking the ACT and feeling extremely nervous and stressed as it is such a big test. Then, the first reading passage was a story about the Grateful Dead, and since he was a big fan, this made me feel like it was my dad being there with me and allowed me to relax during the test." It's these experiences that Cat recognizes as a gentle nod from her dad.

ANNE NELSON

Anne Nelson sees and takes comfort in the signs she receives from her father. Her dad was a lover of the Beatles, and whenever one of their songs comes on, Anne instantly feels his presence.

Anne also looks to nature for signs. She enjoys being outdoors, and whenever she sees a cardinal flying around, she thinks that her dad is sending the bird for her.

"It's a little reminder that he is always with me."

There seemed to be a sense of peace over Anne as she reminisced over these signs. It's as if these moments bring her peace of mind, despite her loss.

REBECCA ASARO

Rebecca Asaro has had encounters since her dad died that would give anyone chills. Not long after her dad passed away, Rebecca's mom made memorial bracelets for the firehouse that included all the names of those they lost. Following 9/11, Rebecca's aunt went on a skiing trip in upstate New York and met a firefighter from another house on the way there. Having close ties to the firefighting community herself, Rebecca's aunt felt moved to speak with him. As she made her way over, he recognized the bracelet on her wrist.

The metal, horseshoe-shaped bracelet was distinctive and a piece that many 9/11 Survivors wear to this day. The man mentioned that he had lost people in his firehouse on 9/11. Rebecca's aunt asked him if he had also received a bracelet like the one she wore so proudly. The man revealed he did, but that he had lost it. Filled with compassion, Rebecca's aunt gave him her own bracelet.

Rebecca didn't know how this small gesture would impact her family until several years later. In December of 2019, Rebecca was at her station when the doorbell rang. It was a firefighter from another firehouse hoping to use their restroom.

"I let him in and then we got to talking when he asked me my name. I told him 'Rebecca Asaro' and his eyes lit up. He asked, 'Are you related to Carl Asaro?'"

The man pulled a bracelet off of his wrist. He was the firefighter Rebecca's aunt had met almost twenty years ago on the skiing trip. He'd been wearing it all this time. The man said he'd been searching for Rebecca and her family for years so that he could return the bracelet. He had known that they were also firefighters but didn't know how to find them. Now, fate had finally brought them together.

Rebecca shares, "It's moments like this where I like to think my dad is with me."

These signs have continued in Rebecca's life, with the most recent one coming in an unusual way. Rebecca signed into Instagram one day and couldn't believe her eyes. Her messages had blown up with hundreds of notifications. As she sifted through, she found that her followers were alerting her of an Instagram story that mentions her dad. Actress Kate Hudson had posted in her story about a bracelet she had received right after 9/11. It reads: "In Memory of Carl Asaro, FDNY."

Kate posted the video to let the family know what she had discovered. What may have been an ordinary moment organizing her jewelry felt like something more. In the video, Kate says, "I feel like it's his way of saying 'I love you' to his kids."

Rebecca and her family were thankful for Kate's message, and felt that their dad had orchestrated this goosebump-worthy experience in some way.

THE NEXT RIGHT THING

As Jon and I have been together, I've started to see and experience many of the signs mentioned by these 9/11 Surviving Children in my own life. I don't think I truly understood the impact of these moments until Jon and I were faced with the difficult decision around moving to Florida. We loved our life in Pennsylvania. We had built a life there, and our family was there. But I dreamed of working for Disney, and Jon had been a Cast Member years before on the Disney College Program.

After Jon and I got married and I received my undergraduate degree, I started interviewing for Professional Internships for The Walt Disney Company. At Disney, you can only apply for a Professional Internship if you are in school or are less than six months graduated, so this was my last chance. Even though Jon had been a Cast Member before and loved it, he wasn't too keen on the idea of moving. His family enjoys living near one another, and this would take him away from that. Making this decision also meant leaving the jobs and friends we loved. A change like this would surely rip us out of our comfort zone.

For better or worse, we put off making the decision until "if" I got the job, never believing that I might actually get it. The indecision and discontent around having to make a choice at all hung in the air between us. Tensions were high. That all changed when I received the email that I'd been accepted for the job. Of all dates, this email arrived on September 11, 2015. I don't believe in mere coincidences and knew in my heart that this was a sign that moving to Florida was the next right thing for us.

My jaw dropped when I read the email. Ironically enough, we were house hunting at the time, and were about to step into the door of a home when I received it. This fact alone is proof that we were still convinced that our lives would remain in Pennsylvania. I laughed in the middle of the street in disbelief and handed Jon the phone. He read the email for himself and said, "I guess we're moving to Florida!"

Both Jon and I knew in that moment that I had to take this job. Yes, accepting this role had a fair share of risks. I had already secured a full-time, salaried job with benefits in Pennsylvania, something I would need to step away from and pick up my life for a six-month internship. But it was the next right thing for our family.

"This was from Dad," Jon said, and the feeling that his dad was looking over us was all we needed to take the next step.

I often think about what our lives might look like if we hadn't taken that leap of faith or if we had ignored that sign. Many times, we would look at each other and say, "What would we be doing if we lived in Pennsylvania right now?" We smile, laugh, and remember. But not for one moment do we regret this decision. Not for one moment do we wish for a different outcome. We did the next right thing, and it led us to our beautiful lives.

I used to feel guilt and shame around getting what I felt were signs for me from Jon's dad. After all, I never knew his father, so how could these be for me?

I didn't know him, but I know my husband. In knowing Jon, his family, and the stories they share, I get to experience even just the tiniest glimpse of who he was. Their lives provide a window into the man he was.

Some people try to play these signs off as the Baader-Meinhof phenomenon. According to health writer Ann Pietrangelo, "Baader-Meinhof phenomenon, or Baader-Meinhof effect, is when your awareness of something increases. This leads you to believe it's actually happening more, even if that's not the case" (Pietrangelo 2019).

For instance, have you ever purchased a car model and happened to see that same car everywhere you go? It could be said that experiences like seeing 9:11 on the clock are following that same frequency illusion. I know in my heart it's more than that, and that it isn't something to ignore.

Now I know better than to not trust these whispers and signs. I've seen the power they have on my life, and I do all I can to step into them wholeheartedly.

EMBRACING THE SIGNS AS A BRIDGE TO RECOVERY

Remembering a parent through the connections their families perceive gives many 9/11 Surviving Children a sense of relationship with their lost loved one. When I relate this with my own infertility, I think about all of the sweet babies that could have been. I also think about Jon's dad and the grandparents that we both lost last year. I imagine that they are all there, cheering us on and waiting until the day we hold our own child in our arms.

According to Litsa Williams, continuing the bonds with the people we've lost can be an important part of the recovery process. She mentions that talking to or imagining conversations with your lost loved one can help provide comfort and clarity.

"Big decisions are often overwhelming, and when you have lost the person who you would have talked it over with, it can be especially hard. Imagining a conversation with them, what they would have said, and the advice they might have given can help us feel connected and also help make big life choices a little easier." (Williams 2021)

For my husband, these signs have helped him immensely in his decision making.

"When I get the feeling that my dad is watching over us, I remember to think, 'What would my dad want me to do in this moment?'"

Many 9/11 Surviving Children have mentioned to me that they try to live their lives in a way that will make their lost parent proud. Litsa mentions this practice as healing for those grieving.

"Be it a spouse, a parent, grandparent, child, or friend, we often struggle knowing our loved one won't be there for accomplishments and milestones. Taking time to recognize that your loved one would be proud of you for a specific accomplishment can be comforting and remind us how we continue to be connected to our loved one" (Williams 2021).

If you've lost someone, an important part of recovery may be taking to heart that the person is with you in spirit or lives on in your memory. At the very least, asking questions of what you can do today to honor them may assist in recovery. How can your actions be inspired by the memory of your loved one? What can you start doing or stop doing today that would make your loved one proud? For my husband, this has always meant living his life to the fullest and not taking one moment for granted. For myself, it means giving myself a little grace and reminders that my infertility is not my fault.

The thing is, bad things can, and will, happen to us. Many times, these things are outside of our control. Losing a parent in 9/11, living through COVID-19, or experiencing infertility aren't necessarily things we signed up for or did something to deserve. There are so many times I ask, "What is God's will for me?" or "What is Jon's dad's will for us?" The more I jump in and do the next right thing, whether that be from a sign I've received, a gut feeling, or from dedicated prayer time, the more discernment I feel. And even if the door is slammed in my face, I know that there are always new doors, leading to the next right thing after that.

POSTTRAUMATIC GROWTH

———

While the tragedy of 9/11 is still with these young adults today, it has also provided a pathway for them to grow from their grief and lead the way in inspiring others. As I've navigated my own personal struggles this year, the triumph from tragedy that I've observed from 9/11 Surviving Children draws me in, wondering how I can bottle these experiences to help myself and others navigate challenges.

BOUNCE FORWARD

I'm very fortunate in that I experienced very little pain and suffering in my childhood. As the oldest of five kids in a middle-class family, it may have seemed from the outside that we would have had to make compromises. The truth is, I wanted for nothing. And above that, things always just seemed to work out for me. My mom would always say if I stepped in shit, I would find a hundred-dollar bill.

While I always resented that phrase, I can now acknowledge the truth in it. With an always-on, type A personality, failure wasn't an option, nor was it something I often experienced. This isn't meant as a humblebrag, but rather an insight into how little adversity I faced as a child. My parents always told me I could do anything I put my mind to, and I believed them—until I tried to get pregnant.

I believe that lack of adversity in my youth has caused me heartache as an adult. My biggest challenges in life began at the age of twenty-five, and I can't say I've always taken them in stride. There's no doubt that infertility has changed me. There are days I question my purpose and would rather not get out of bed. Days where the thought of one more appointment or medication is suffocating. Days where I cannot see the end of this barren season.

But when I see how Jon and other 9/11 Surviving Children have dealt with their grief, it gives me hope. They've survived 100 percent of the days they've lived past 9/11, and in many ways, they've thrived. Funny enough, this same optimism and ability to bounce back are what gave me the most agita when we started our journey to baby Lynch. Jon was going through this battle with me in the midst of being laid off and yet our reactions were completely different.

There were many times I have asked him, "Why can't you just be angry *with* me?" As I took a closer look, I softened my heart and saw that there was something to learn from this. I recognized that this was something I could tap into to help myself and others.

While the children of 9/11 were my main focus group, I was curious to see how this resilience might play out with others who also experienced great tragedy in their lives. Stacie Boyar, who worked with many impacted by the Marjory Stoneman Douglas High School shooting, had interesting insights to share on the topic.

I was most intrigued by Boyar's story of the young girl who experienced symptoms of PTSD just by hearing about someone else's experience. This retelling was enough for the young girl to begin having trauma of her own associated with the event.

At first, I was shocked to hear that such a thing was possible, but it makes sense. Thinking back to 9/11, there was collective grief we felt as a nation that day even if we didn't personally lose anyone in the event. As I reflect on my own memories of 9/11, I recognize how difficult it must have been for my parents to try to explain to their second-grader what was going on in a city they've never been to, all without showing the fear that they were experiencing. While traumatic, that shared empathy made us a more united nation—arguably, since the attack on Pearl Harbor.

The same can be said for the community of Parkland, Florida. While pain and suffering is a huge part of their journey, action and unity is there too.

"A lot of success stories have come from this loss. Most notably, many of the children who attended Stoneman Douglas at the time of the event started March For Our Lives, which was a huge undertaking."

March For Our Lives is on a mission "to harness the power of young people across the country to fight for sensible gun violence prevention policies that save lives." The organization is "created by survivors, so you don't have to be one," a powerful message in a time when mass gun violence continues to plague our nation (March For Our Lives 2020).

Beyond organizing at the national level, the children of Stoneman Douglas have remained loyal to their communities.

According to Stacie Boyar, "Many of the families of children who survived the shooting were privileged enough to be able to move following the events. The parents offered this option to their kids, but most of them opted to go back to Stoneman Douglas despite witnessing such a horrible tragedy there."

These successes are not meant at all to belittle the negative impacts felt as a part of PTSD, but rather to showcase that there are some positive benefits at play as well. This "growth from grief" process is called posttraumatic growth (PTG), and I had an inkling that it might play an interesting role in the lives of 9/11 Surviving Children as well.

Boyar shares, "Posttraumatic growth is the growth someone experiences after a trauma. It can manifest in many ways, often meaning stronger relationships with those around them, heightened self-esteem, and a sense of deeper purpose for their lives."

Over time, people reap benefits from their challenges. Since it takes that time for this growth to marinate, the children of 9/11 are reaching the peak of their posttraumatic growth potential. This realization is when I finally understood my husband isn't bouncing back. He's bouncing *forward*.

HOW DO WE GROW?

When facing adversity, posttraumatic growth can lead to better awareness of one's vulnerability and limitations. Doing so may be the driving force behind the children of 9/11 sharing and growing from their stories. Their identity, while not strangled by their loss, blossoms in spite of it.

So how do the rest of us move from PTSD to PTG? Or rather, how do we embrace that PTSD and PTG likely exist together?

For many who experience tragedy or loss, spiraling negative thoughts keep us stuck and spinning our wheels. I've noticed this for myself, as when I tend to have one negative thought, it is soon followed by another. And then another. And before I know it, I've spent thirty minutes pulling myself down into a rabbit hole of worries that most likely won't even happen.

If this is you too, you're not alone. Lucky for us, Boyar shares some ways on how we can start retraining our brains.

"For those that are good at visualization, you can try visualizing a stop sign whenever negative thoughts pop up. I've had clients who wear a rubber band or even a hair tie on their wrist. When they have a negative thought, they snap it to literally snap themselves out of those thoughts."

I shared some of my own challenges with Boyar on how there are days where I struggle to find anything I'm grateful for. I even feel guilty as I share this experience, because I recognize how many blessings I have in my life! This became so challenging for me that by the fall of 2020, I cried thinking about Thanksgiving out of fear that I'd be asked to share what I'm thankful for; just the thought of the activity made me sick to my stomach. Luckily, Boyar was able to share some techniques with me on how to lead with an attitude of gratitude.

"Having gratitude is an essential part of recovery. Some days you won't want to, but it's waking up every day and thinking of at least one thing you're grateful for. If you can't think of anything, just take a breath and listen. It could be as simple as, 'I'm grateful I hear the birds chirping outside,' but finding something to start your day positively even before stepping out of bed is essential. It will help to set the tone for the day."

I wanted to give Boyar's advice a test run, so I started keeping a gratitude journal. Every night before bed, I sit with my husband and write down three things we are grateful for that day. It felt silly and awkward for me at first, but I quickly began to feel like myself again. By settling my mind on the things I do have, I found myself less worried about what I don't have. This practice has drastically changed everything, from how I sleep to how I go about my day.

REFINED BY FIRE

During the time I had with both Stacie Boyar and K. Thomas, I couldn't help but feel like I was experiencing a much-needed therapy session. Their caring demeanors gave me a safe space to ask openly and freely about how to combat my own challenges while also navigating what we can learn from other people's experiences.

My interview with K. Thomas was where I really felt I came to understand PTG at its core.

We talked a lot about the image of the Phoenix and how it represents the idea of renewal after adversity. It means recognizing that the journey doesn't end with tragedy.

Nothing done well happens without refinement. There is often a difficult process of applying pressure and heat before something beautiful can emerge. To rise from the ashes is to step into the cycle of refinement and to not stop walking until you've emerged from the fire.

K told me, "We don't grow when we are comfortable. If you're in that place of discomfort—keep going."

Finally, I understood the difference between Jon and me. I was experiencing that place of discomfort for the first time, and I didn't know what to do with it. I despised it, rejected it, pretended it wasn't there. Jon knows better. He's been there before, and he has seen the beauty of refinement by fire. He knows the secret that I didn't—that there is another side to this so beautiful that we'd walk through this hell time and time again to get there.

That discomfort you feel during challenging times? You *must* lean into it! That feeling is the catalyst for great change and growth in your life.

THE TRIUMPH

When seeing the data and information about the impacts of PTSD, it's easy to see why I struggled to understand how my husband, who experienced such hardship in his childhood, became the joyful and optimistic person he is. I wanted to see how those I spoke to were able to go from surviving to living the fullest life possible.

As I continued my interviews, I wondered if any of them would be using the techniques recommended by Stacie Boyar and K. Thomas to cope with their tragedy and grow from it. What we see next are their personal experiences with triumphantly rising. Their distinct ability to dust themselves off is seen through all moments, big and small, as they navigate the rest of their lives. As you dive in with us, I hope you'll uncover even the tiniest nuggets of wisdom to add to your tool belt.

JON LYNCH

The resilience and strength I see in my husband is the reason I wanted to write this book in the first place. I knew that these traits didn't just come to him overnight. It had to be years of practicing a certain way of being. As Jon thinks back to how he was able to bounce forward, it's the time with his family that sticks out the most. On days where they would be honoring his father, you could find Jon's family gathered together, doing something fun to celebrate his memory.

Whether it be hiking, flying a kite, or seeing a Broadway show, Jon feels that "his dad would want that"—his whole family enjoying their time. They don't always have to talk about their dad for it to be a special moment, but if they are, you can bet it's Jon who is doing the talking. Jon has always felt a responsibility to share his vivid memories of his dad with his brothers in hopes of helping them know him as Jon did. Sharing the memories and the stories is one way Jon pulls himself out of the darkness of trauma and into the light of his triumph.

But it's not just the big moments where Jon calls on his memories of his dad to heal. It's in the little, everyday decisions. Sometimes he'll even imagine having a conversation with his dad to determine the next steps he can take. This helps him find peace in the choices he's had to make. He wants so badly to make his dad proud. I tell him all the time that he is, but maybe even more importantly, Jon should be proud of himself, too.

Jon is also someone who can truly make something out of nothing. While I'm lucky if I can correctly paint a solid color, Jon's artistic abilities are far-reaching. From visual to performing arts, there really isn't anything Jon tries that he isn't good at. I've never seen the man use a stencil, and yet he creates the most incredible drawings. Even when he learned how to stilt walk for his parade performer job at Disney, the leaders applauded him for needing no time at the safety bar. He is extremely gifted in many areas, and taps into these talents as a way of healing.

Jon says, "I like how I feel when I'm creating something, and I find myself escaping to that place when I need a pick-me-up."

It is not lost on Jon that he gained many things when he lost his dad. None of these things bring back his dad, but they've shaped his life in a way that would look quite different had his dad never passed. Whether it be money or experience, Jon remains grateful for every minute. Instead of being bitter, Jon embraces what he has and keeps on bouncing forward.

This truth became abundantly clear to me the first time Jon provided an interview (other than for this book) about his experience with 9/11. A podcaster had reached out to me, hoping to connect with 9/11 Surviving Children to speak with them about their journeys. I put a few feelers out there, trying to be respectful of the fact that many of them get asked to share extremely often. A few obliged, including Jon and his brother Mark. I was home at the time of Jon's interview, and I couldn't help but sit with my back to the door of my office, where he sat to take the call.

The podcaster asked if Jon ever wished his dad didn't go back in the building that day. I held my breath during the silence and waited for Jon's answer. Then, in a way so distinct to who Jon is, he spoke his truth.

"Of course," he said. "But that's not who he was. And there are people alive today who had something important to do and are here to do it because of him."

I immediately broke out into tears. It took every ounce of energy in my body to pick myself up off the floor and restrain the wailing sounds that came from my mouth. This statement isn't just something that Jon said because he thinks it sounds nice. He believes this truth down to his very core. For him to be able to stand so firmly on this truth is a testimony to what the power of positive thinking can do.

MARK LYNCH

Even while Mark recognized at a young age that his family was different, he feels grateful for the experiences he did have and feels that he has been luckier than most.

"I know a lot of times not having a father figure in the home with young children can be really detrimental. As a testament to both my mom and the community around us, it wasn't that much of a hindrance in our life. Sure, it affected us, but it wasn't a developmental hindrance."

For Mark, there is no "life before 9/11" or "life with Dad" to look back on, and he recognizes how much his mom had to do in order to give him a "normal" life. And while I wasn't there when Mark's mom was raising him, I've seen and heard the ways she cares for her children. I know how many resources went into ensuring that her kids were always properly cared for, nurtured, and provided for. From access to mental health professionals, camps, and quality education, there was no stone she'd leave unturned for them.

I see it even in the way she has shown up for me as my step-mother-in-law. There has never been a time where I couldn't call on her for advice. Her dedication to ensuring that I don't put my foot in my mouth while writing this book has shown me how much she cares not only about these stories but about her kids.

In the day-to-day moments where the children of 9/11 are less than grateful (because let's be honest, I'm not sure I know anyone who is completely immune to taking our loved ones for granted), I hope that Surviving Parents like my step-mother-in-law get to hear and see sentiments like the one

Mark shared of his mom. They deserve to know that their efforts do not go unappreciated.

Mark feels that their proximity to New York also helped others to understand the situation and ensure they got the help they needed. "There were support groups made up of other widows and their families, and I recall many of my friends' dads stepping in and being significant male figures in my life."

Raising a family of three boys as a single parent does take a village, and luckily Mark's family has found, and has access to, an incredible community.

MATTHEW BOCCHI

Matthew Bocchi also credits his family for helping to survive during his most challenging times. After they learned of the sexual abuse he suffered at the hands of his uncle, his family encouraged him to share with law enforcement. This led to a conviction that gave Matthew some peace of mind while helping him to find healing and a pathway forward after addiction.

Matthew has a strong call to action to others looking for the triumph in their lives:

"My message to other children of 9/11 victims would be to come forward and talk about your experiences and what's bothering you. ... It gets better and you should maintain hope that it gets better. I thought it would be a life filled with drug and alcohol abuse. ... I didn't think I would get sober and I thought I would be constantly trying to melt away the emotions, the guilt and the shame. Now I pretty much have a life full of peace and serenity. Not every day is amazing, but it's better than it used to be." (Robinson 2021).

Matthew's story is a resounding reminder that even when things seem like they won't ever get better, even a mustard seed of faith can see you through to the other side. When I had the chance to speak with Matthew myself, he mentioned that one of the teachings he has taken with him from his time in Alcoholics Anonymous (AA) is that a "spiritual awakening" is important for recovery. His first sign from his dad—the fly—was the moment things changed for him. Matthew continues to call on his dad as he works every day to maintain his sobriety.

The signs he received from his father, along with renewed inspiration by his legacy, helped Matthew write his memoir. Matthew describes writing *Sway* as a cathartic experience, and the more he shares his story, the better he feels.

PETE DAVIDSON

For Pete Davidson, his growth manifested into his incredible comedic talent. Pete certainly got a head start on honing his craft. His mom began driving him to Manhattan comedy clubs from their home in Staten Island where he began doing stand-up as early as sixteen years old (Nededog 2015).

Pete credits the challenges he faced in his childhood for his fearlessness in his acts. "There's nothing I won't joke about, and I think it's because of what happened to me," he said. "That's the worst thing that could ever happen to somebody. Now it's just like, 'Who cares, man?'" (Nededog 2015).

One can imagine that finding the funny in 9/11 wasn't easy to do in the days after the attack. *The Daily Show* went off the air for nine days. Many remember the *Saturday Night Live* episode that aired eighteen days later, with Lorne Michaels asking NYC Mayor Rudy Giuliani if they can be funny. Even *The Onion*, the paper known for its satirical articles, struggled with words.

Pete seems to enjoy living in that space where it's uncomfortable and unclear if the topic is a laughing matter. He shares himself that, "I like making things that are dark, awkward, weird things that you don't really find funny, funny."

In a time where our nation was walking on eggshells, laughter may have been the best medicine. Psychologist Daniela S. Hugelshofer suggests that humor acts as a buffer against depression and hopelessness (Khazan 2014). This would imply that humor cannot happen without pain as a catalyst. Mark Twain said it best when he expressed that, "The secret source of humor itself is not joy, but sorrow. There is no humor in heaven." (Khazan 2014).

ALEXA EDWARDS

As the global pandemic has changed our world, Alexa Edwards recognizes that her experiences have given her wisdom around life and loss. Some of that wisdom includes how Alexa recognizes how challenging this time has been for everyone and acknowledges everyone's pain as very real and valid.

Losing her dad at such a young age showed her that sometimes life hands you the short end of the stick, but you have a choice to keep moving forward. While 2020 was certainly challenging and life-altering for Alexa too, she brings a unique perspective, recognizing that what she has conquered already has prepared her for conquering the next challenge.

The way Alexa sees it, the pandemic is just another mountain to climb out of the many she's already faced. Regretting what "could have been" had there not been a pandemic or had she not lost her father isn't the space where Alexa chooses to live. Instead, she faces her challenges head-on, grateful for what it is she does have.

Alexa's triumph comes in finding healthy outlets for her to express herself through her trials. As a dancer, Alexa uses movement as a way of releasing and letting go. Like a warm, fuzzy blanket, dance is the one thing Alexa knew she could count on—or so she thought.

As a recent graduate at UNC, Alexa Edwards is right on the cusp of taking on the world. And while college might seem like an academic safety net before entering the "real world," the pandemic has made it anything but that. Alexa recently suffered from a broken nose and concussion, and the security she found in her ability to dance was stripped away from her. This time required Alexa to do some serious reflection as she struggled with the realization that many things that happen in our lives are out of our control.

Alexa recently developed a practice to help her set better expectations when challenges arise. She begins by identifying the items over which she has influence. Everything not on this list goes in a "cannot control" bucket. Alexa now spends her time focusing on those areas of influence, making the most of those opportunities and letting go of the rest.

Alexa is growing every day in the discovery of herself and her emotions, which can be challenging when others commend her for her stoic front.

"You're so happy! You have it all together, even after all you've been through!" are sentiments that Alexa often hears. And while she takes great pride in this, it has also empowered her to put up a front that everything is okay, even when it's not. Alexa is determined to keep breaking down those walls and being honest with herself and others about how she is doing.

THE BURNETT SISTERS

The Burnett sisters are clearly influenced and inspired by the legacy their dad leaves behind. The family speaks very openly about their loss and, more importantly, the steps their dad Thomas took to fight for his nation. Their mother, Deena, has traveled the world speaking to many about the heroism her husband displayed that day.

While being so open can invite a lot of unwanted attention, it has also become a cathartic experience for the family. Though it's evident the impact her father has had on her life, Halley credits her mother as being one of the biggest influences. With tears in her eyes, Halley described to me how her mom is just as much of a hero as her dad.

"The world knows my dad is a hero, but no one knows my mom is."

That statement hit me right in the gut. There Halley was, pouring out her soul to me about the incredible mother who raised her.

In the midst of the greatest loss of her life, their mother— Deena Burnett—poured her love out onto others. She continues to give her time and money to those in need, and her daughters emulate her behavior. They see her as a role model, and often look for ways that they can become more like their mother.

As you've seen already, this is not an uncommon sentiment amongst 9/11 Surviving Children. Oftentimes, it's the Surviving Parent who, despite all odds, held together the pieces that were so crucial to their kids' development. From keeping routines to securing access to recovery programs, the 9/11 Surviving Parents are the hidden heroes.

REBECCA ASARO

After years of training, Rebecca and her brother Marc graduated from the FDNY academy in September 2019. But the Asaro family firefighting legacy doesn't stop there. They joined their two other brothers, Matthew and Carl Jr., who are also FDNY firefighters. Rebecca's uncle is also a firefighter. Together they found a common purpose: doing a job they love and honoring their dad.

"People will come to my house and they just can't believe how well me and my siblings get along. We bring the camaraderie of the firehouse wherever we go. We play pranks on each other, leaving notes and things at each other's firehouses. It's funny how far we've come, together."

Rebecca enjoys that she can now give back to her community through her role as a firefighter, but that isn't the only way she's been able to help others through the years. In the summer of 2002, America's Camp opened to create a safe haven for the children of those who died on 9/11. The hope was that they'd find ways to cope with their loss while also forming friendships with others who lived the same tragedy. Rebecca recalls great memories and friendships from her time at camp, but especially remembers her time assisting as a counselor.

Once Rebecca and her peers aged out of the camp, they offered it another summer for the children of Newton, CT, where a mass shooting at Sandy Hook Elementary School happened on December 14, 2012. The shooting left twenty children and six adults dead (CNN 2012). Rebecca is grateful that these camp experiences continue to exist as a way to support others who experience tragedy at a young age.

THE THOMAS SISTERS

The challenges that the Thomas sisters walked through in their early lives prepared them for future trials and helped them be a friend to others in need.

Rose has Acute Intermittent Porphyria, a rare genetic metabolic disorder that can cause symptoms such as abdominal pain, nausea, vomiting, constipation, pain from muscle weakness, hallucinations, seizures, and insomnia. The condition once kept her in the hospital for a month.

"My grandma calls me her little warrior and everyone says I remind them of my dad. My dad was brave and he inspires me. I like to think that I'm a fighter like him. Because he died when I was at such a young age and I've learned how to grow up without a dad, I've matured more than other kids my age because they didn't have to live without a parent."

Bridget has been able to help others cope with their trauma because of her own experiences. She recalls being in college when a friend of hers lost her dad to suicide. One day they were together at the gym and her friend asked," How do you do it?"

Bridget thought she was talking about how to use the elliptical, but her friend meant something else. "No, how do you deal with not having your dad?" At that point in time, her friend hadn't confided in anyone else about the pain she had been dealing with since her dad's suicide.

Because Bridget had been open about her loss and all she'd gone through, she was able to help a friend in need. Bridget shared that while the pain of losing a parent never really goes away, it does become more manageable and that there is help. While doing so didn't make her friend's problem disappear, it gave her hope. After years of searching for hope of her own, Bridget was elated to pass it on.

MARIA GARCIA

Despite her PTSD diagnosis, Maria Garcia has managed to find healthy ways to manage her symptoms. For Maria, learning to talk about the things that bother her has helped her immensely.

"The more I talked about the themes I was having in my nightmares and the triggers I had, the less my mind saw them as triggers."

Comfort objects have also played a large role in Maria's recovery. As a sensory person, she enjoys finding objects that are soft and scratchy. From pillows to stuffed animals, the act of pushing into these items helps Maria to reground herself. Even the thought of these items seemed to bring Maria joy, as, during the interview, she outstretched her hands and demonstrated the way she might cuddle up to one of these items. It made me want to reach for the closest soft object myself!

Sensory and physical elements for healing seem to be a common theme for Maria as she also activates this technique on the stage. Spending time in theatre was one of the first therapeutic opportunities Maria had to express herself.

She shares that, "The arts were my life! After my dad died, I think I did at least four shows that next year."

Maria found a place where she could be herself while in theatre. There is irony in the fact that an activity that requires you to be someone else actually helps you find yourself. I also wonder if there's a part of Maria that enjoyed the escapism that theatre can provide. Stepping into a fantasy world devoid of the challenges of your own life can be a refreshing experience.

NICOLE FOSTER

Nicole Foster believes that she's been through hell already and can do it again if she has to. The belief that her father was watching over her was also a huge proponent of her positivity during her journey with leukemia.

"During that time, I knew I was safe because my dad was watching over me and making things align for me like the right treatment and doctors I had surrounding me."

Knowing Nicole's background with faith and spirituality, I asked her point-blank if she was ever angry with God with the series of unfortunate events that were thrown her way. She shares that she really didn't have time to think that way. For Nicole, it has always been about putting one foot in front of the other.

"At the time of my diagnosis, it was just a really big shock for me. Every day I just thought, 'I'm going to take everything day by day, so today I am going to take this treatment.' I never really focused on what was going to happen six months from then."

Nicole has also made great strides with her anxiety. She is able to see the benefits of a well-balanced life—from nutrition; to exercise; to mental health.

"I've come to realize that anxiety is a natural response to trauma. I work really hard to take care of my mental health and practice meditation and breath work, even when it's not something that's coming easily for me ... I think it just comes down to reminding myself that I'm in the present moment. Although bad things have happened in my life, whatever awful thing that I'm thinking of that day, odds are that it's not going to happen. So, I just have to lean into the other side of it and say, 'Probably not going to happen, there is no point wasting

my time thinking about this,' and encourage myself to let go of
that thought and move on. I also try to remind myself that my
dad is guiding me and protecting me, so I lean on my faith in
that way. It's not something that always comes easily for me,
but I do find comfort knowing my dad is there for me. A lot
of it is trust that things are going to unfold the way that they
should and that things are going to be okay in the end."

Trust. This concept is at the center of Nicole's triumph.
As she trusts that all things are aligning for her good, she
rests easier in that truth.

ANNE NELSON

Anne Nelson found the support of the recovery resources to
be crucial as she worked through her challenges. Both Anne
and her sister Caitlin attended America's Camp as a way of
healing. The camp experience was one where they finally felt
like they weren't alone in their grief.

"It was the one place where I felt I could truly be a kid. I
didn't have to worry about other children treating me differently just because I was a '9/11 kid.' Labels didn't exist at
America's Camp, and that was so refreshing."

When Anne lost her sister, she was already an adult, and
camp was no longer an option.

"I ended up finding a group called the Dinner Party. You
attend with people who have had similar losses. You can find
tables to join with people who lost a parent, or sibling, or both.
These types of groups were an essential part of my healing."

Anne felt seen and heard in these groups, providing her
a safe space to express herself and continue her journey in
bouncing forward.

WE ARE NOT WHAT HAPPENS TO US

There's a lot to unpack in the ways these 9/11 Surviving Children have been triumphant. There is also significant overlap in what worked for one person vs. another. From comfort objects; to spirituality; to an outlet in the arts; to the ability to help others—9/11 Surviving Children have stepped out of their trials and into their triumph. They've grown beyond the tragedy and have bounced forward, finding ways that they can use these experiences for good.

Even with the common bonds we find in these stories, every person is unique in their experiences. What works for one may not work for the other. I think the recovery tactics represented here can be thought of as getting dressed in the morning. You might try a few things on and realize that they aren't the right fit and toss them to the side. In the same way, you might try some of these techniques and realize they aren't for you. After ripping through your entire closet, there is no greater relief than finally finding what fits you perfectly. The right outfit often includes several pieces that complement one another, just as it's often a combination of several techniques that create the perfect blend.

In this same way, I hope you are able to parse out what might work for you in this stage of your journey. May their tales of triumph equip and encourage you that the same is possible in your life! It is not what happens to us, it's how we respond to each moment. When we take control of our minds, when we lay all things down and *trust*, the possibilities for life are endless.

FINDING MY OWN TRIUMPHS

———

I recently saw a drawing that I thought well represented what it is to grow beyond tragedy. The illustration showed three jars of the same size, each with a ball inside. The ball is grief; the jar is our lives. The ball inside the first jar is large, with a medium and small ball in the second and third. This represents how we often believe that grief shrinks over time.

The next illustration showed three jars: small, medium, and large. Each jar has a ball of the same size in them. This represents how the grief itself doesn't get any smaller, but that we actually grow *around* our grief. We find purpose and meaning in it. We make space for new experiences, and our grief becomes more manageable.

As I've conducted these interviews, I've been able to take away insights that have helped my jar to grow. My hope in these pages is that you are able to identify the crossover between my own personal experience and the experience of 9/11 Surviving Children in a way that allows your own jar to grow.

LAUGHING IT OFF

I'm not Pete Davidson funny, but I like to think I have a knack for making people laugh. As life has continued to throw its curveballs at me, my humor has definitely gotten darker.

Case in point: if you know my husband, you'll know that he blows his nose so obnoxiously. Doesn't matter what time of day or if his allergies are acting up or not. His honker is unreal. It's the wake-up call that starts our day. It's like a cruise ship pulling into port. It is a true medical marvel.

I have asked Jon if he would like to visit an ENT to see if there is something we could do about it. He refuses. So I am left, day in and day out, listening to that big old nose of his. Recently I've been blaming that nose on our infertility, joking with anyone who will hear it that God knows better than to allow us to procreate and pass on that fabulous gene. Most people cringe as they laugh along with me. They aren't sure what to say because they know the joke comes from a painful place. For better or for worse, I've been using this humor to help cope with my tragedy.

Dr. Peter McGraw—professor at the University of Colorado, Boulder, director of the Humor Research Lab, and co-author of *The Humor Code: A Global Search for What Makes Things Funny*—says that "The act of making jokes is about transforming these violations and transforming them into something that is laugh-worthy. It allows us the opportunity to see situations differently." (Sloat 2019).

Dr. Peter McGraw also explains that when we laugh, we experience positive emotions. When we hear the punch line of a joke we resonate with, the brain releases dopamine, serotonin, and endorphins which leaves us feeling good (Sloat 2019).

I recognize that trying to laugh about my circumstances is one way I'm navigating my grief. What I'm cautious of, though, is allowing that humor to mask how I'm really feeling. By making a joke of it, I keep people at bay. How could I possibly be hurting if I'm making people laugh? Revealing my true emotional state is where the vulnerability comes in, and when you're vulnerable, shit gets real. Sometimes I think I don't really want shit to get real. I don't want people to know that I'm human, too, and am struggling.

When I notice myself getting to that deeply cynical, joking place, I check my mental state. I ask myself the question, "Is this a healthy response that will make myself and others laugh? Or is this an effort to put up more walls?"

It seems that many comedians struggle when their jokes come from the latter. I wonder if Pete Davidson is doing the same? Is he using comedy to deal with the loss of his father, or is he comedic *because* of the loss of his father? Given his circumstances, Pete could have very easily fallen into the same traps that other *SNL* comedians have. Take John Belushi and Chris Farley as an example. Both men died at the age of thirty-three from drug overdoses. And in many ways, Pete toes a fine line himself with his own drug usage.

Was it the party lifestyle that sucked them in? Or was there a deeper, emotional issue that was leading them to use? Was their comedic genius a result of some dark, internal conflict? There's not much we know about Belushi and Farley's personal lives for us to make a clear judgment of what led to this behavior.

Stanton Peele—a psychologist and psychotherapist who specializes in addiction—has one theory. He concludes that many who, as he says, "actively try to kill themselves" (in this case through the use of drugs) have deep-rooted issues that began in their childhood.

Peele shares, "I think it is unavoidable that the sources of such self-destruction be discovered in childhood experiences at home. People only learn to hate themselves when those on whom they count for their earliest support and respect instead teach them that they are worthless or despicable. When a child has learned this message, he may spend the rest of his life trying to prove it is true and reacting with discomfort to any information or person which says it is not true. Ultimately, he may achieve the punishment he seems to feel he deserves." (Stanton, 1982).

Could it be that what holds successful 9/11 Surviving Children together is a strong unit of family and friends? I can only say one thing for certain—it is my support system that is holding me together right now. Without them, I honestly wonder what destructive behavior I'd be getting myself into. But that's what good families (and friends) do. They hold you when you fall. They walk with you through the tough parts. Then they rise with you. And they laugh at your stupid and borderline inappropriate jokes.

MORE THAN JUST TEDDY BEARS

It's not just good family and friends that get me through the tough days; it's the techniques and tricks that I've learned from the many 9/11 Surviving Children I've spoken to, some of which I realized I was already doing on my own and only needed to further home in on these skills. When Maria mentioned how she uses comfort objects, I immediately thought, "I have one of those!"

If you were to visit me in my at-home, pandemic-approved office during a stressful meeting, you may be able to tell right away what this item is. With my hair tied in a messy bun, you can usually find me intently listening to the challenges with a ball of Play-Doh in hand. As I kneed my hands into the dough, I feel the wheels in my head turning, and in some ways, slowing. Focusing on the dough and how it feels brings me out of the stressed, anxiety-ridden place and into a place of presence. Yup. Definitely a comfort object.

But how, and why, do comfort objects work? The first example that comes to mind for most is Linus van Pelt and his trusty blue blanket from the *Peanuts* comics. While blankets and bears are meant to be transitional items for kids to eventually grow out of, there are circumstances where adults too can benefit from the psychological benefits.

According to Margaret Van Ackeren, licensed therapist, "In most instances, adults sleep with childhood stuffed animals because it brings them a sense of security and reduces negative feelings, such as loneliness and anxiety." The use of such objects is also recommended for those suffering from grief and trauma to aid with their healing and recovery (Gains 2020).

There is something truly comforting about wrapping your arms around or pressing your hands into a soft item. Hearing about the benefits to my mental health makes me want to squeeze that Play-Doh harder, hold my pets tighter, and bring my favorite stuffed animal a bit closer.

SANCTUARY

If you've seen *The Hunchback of Notre Dame*, the classic Disney animated film, you may remember the scene where Quasimodo holds Esmeralda over his head and shouts "Sanctuary!" I remember it so vividly that when Jon and I went to Paris, we tried to reenact it outside the doors of Notre Dame.

It didn't turn out quite like the movie, but it did make us laugh. Now every time we see that photo, we shout "Sanctuary!" at the top of our lungs.

As I battle the grief that comes along with infertility, I am looking for my sanctuary—that place where no one and nothing can harm me. I want to feel safe and secure.

Whether it be dancing, painting, musical theatre, or beyond, a theme amongst many 9/11 Surviving Children is how the arts showed up for them when they needed them most. They provided a safe place for them in their darkest hour. As a former musical theatre major in college, I resonated with the idea that the arts could help in the healing process from grief and trauma. I know that feeling of having a bad day and getting on stage (whether it be a real stage or the driver's seat of my car) and belting it out. That feeling of the world slipping away as the song wraps you up in its warm embrace is unforgettable.

"After a traumatic loss, the arts allow what can't be spoken about to come into form," says Sharon Strouse, a licensed clinical art therapist (Corrigan 2020). Through the arts, all that pain and heartache has a channel to travel through. Rather than bottled up in your body, the arts allow for movement.

Over the course of the pandemic, my husband has been creating. He kicked me out of my garage gym to set up shop, making anything he could get his hands on. From topiaries to wood lawn cutouts, the pandemic has arguably been the most prolific time of my husband's life.

Jon always had a knack for the arts, even before he lost his dad. He is always proud to tell me how advanced he was, drawing detailed faces—with ears and everything—before other kids were. When his dad died, he took that skill and ran with it. He tried out for every musical and play that his school or community theatre was offering. On stage, he wasn't the 9/11 kid, and there was great freedom in that.

Because he already knew how the arts helped him during challenging times in the past, slipping back to that place when he lost his job due to COVID-19 was easy for him. He could have sat and sulked, saying, "Woe is me." Instead, he picked up a paintbrush. A hammer. A glue gun. Not because he wanted to be *busy*, but because he wanted to be at *peace*. The arts are his sanctuary.

I needed a sanctuary—something I could sink my teeth into and create. I'm extremely grateful to have maintained my job throughout this pandemic, but I missed out on something crucial that many furloughed and laid off people gained: perspective. When my husband wasn't so busy working, he could take the time to ask the question, "Is this really what I want to do with my life?" Many others have done the same, making the pandemic pivot and choosing a new path that allows their creative juices to flow. They found their sanctuaries because they were forced to slow down.

So here I am, writing a book. It's my sanctuary as of now. It's the place I can come to every morning and pour my heart into. It's there for me when I need it. When it's finished, I'll find a new sanctuary. The important part is that I never forget how being in that creative space made me feel better in my darkest days.

WATCH ME

There have been many moments where I would be listening to the journeys of the 9/11 Surviving Children and thinking about my own challenges. My first reaction is guilt and shame. How could I possibly compare my trials to those of someone who lost a parent in 9/11? Someone who has had a cancer diagnosis. Someone who lost her sister and her dad. And yet, there are days when I cannot imagine how I will have to go through this one more day. I keep hearing about this light at the end of the tunnel, but how *long* is the damn tunnel?

The irony is not lost on me that my dad and Jon's dad share a birthday. If my dad and I had a relationship status on Facebook, it would say: "It's complicated." Not wanting to call my dad on his birthday fills me with guilt and shame because of the fact that Jon can't call his. There are moments like this often where I worry that my problems aren't big or valid enough to complain about since I'm married to someone who has managed seemingly bigger ones.

While infertility can in no way, shape, or form be compared with the challenges that 9/11 Surviving Children have faced, I feel that the grief and trials associated with both can be similar. One of the most challenging parts of my journey has been the questioning of my faith. There have been many times throughout this process where I have angrily turned to God and asked, "Why me?" I have felt forgotten, alone, and unworthy. I've asked myself many times what I've done to make God not want me to have children (which is not at all how I believe God works, by the way, but it doesn't stop me from asking and beating myself up over it!).

When Nicole Foster got her cancer diagnosis, she didn't have time to ask, "Why me?" Her life very literally depended on her recovery. I want to be like that! Again, even in that statement, I feel the grief and shame come on. I become angry with myself for being less like Nicole and more like Payton. Instead of kicking myself for playing the victim, I can choose to change my mindset moving forward.

Resilience is less about who you are and more about how you think. Resilience is the shift from thinking "why me" to "*try* me, I've got this ... now watch me!"

MEDITATE

Three years ago, I was diagnosed with acute anxiety disorder. This often comes with excessive thoughts of fear or worry. For me, even being a few minutes late is something that brings me great anxiety. I'm not typically someone who can just "relax," something I am constantly being told will increase my chances of conceiving. So, when some 9/11 Surviving Children shared their own challenges, I wanted to dig deeper to understand how they are working through their anxiety.

Nicole mentioned meditation, and I was quick to dismiss that for myself. After all, meditation is for Zen, centered people, not emotional-rollercoaster people like me. Never did I stop to think that maybe all these meditating people are Zen and centered *because* they are doing meditation.

The biggest challenge I've had with meditating, aside from not being able to sit still in silence for that long, is dealing with my own thoughts. I am quick to judge them or dismiss them. I am easily angered when I drift away from the intended focus or turn negative. But what is that saying about me? Why am I so angry when I'm not doing something perfectly? Why don't I give myself the same grace and patience everyone else would like when they're practicing something new? Now *that's* something to meditate on.

My whole life has been about being successful. The feeling that no one will love me unless I do great things has stuck with me since childhood. This is why I struggle to meditate, be alone with my thoughts, or try something new. I'm crippled by the fear of failure. I started to ask myself, "what's the *worst* thing that could happen here?" I think some negative thoughts? I don't get the job? Someone tells me no? I never become a mom?

I can handle all of those things. I'm already handling some of them. And frankly, most of the worst-case scenarios I imagine most likely won't happen.

Things *will* be okay in the end. And if it's not okay, then it's not the end. While I can't see the finish line yet for my own grief and suffering, and some days it feels like there is no end in sight, I trust that this is only halftime in my story. And while it seems like my team is losing, the victory is on its way. Being reflective in the middle of a struggle is not easy. While I'm not at a stage where I can necessarily be grateful for my struggle, what I can do is have hope for the future. Things won't always be this way.

BELONGING

My mom once shared a story with me of when I was in elementary school. She came in to help as a recess aid one day and found that I was playing by myself while all the other kids were interacting with each other. Little first-grader Payton wasn't great at making friends. That didn't change much as I got older, and I would often come home crying that no one wanted to be my friend. I think of little Payton often, all alone on the playground. How sad she must have been.

Everyone wants to feel like they belong. Humans are designed to find community with others. Sometimes when you're going through circumstances that your closest family and friends don't understand, it's easy to feel like you don't belong.

Seeking out communities like Anne Nelson found in the Dinner Party is one way that 9/11 Surviving Children have found their belonging. I realized there was an opportunity for me to find some of that too.

According to their website, the Dinner Party is a platform for grieving twenty-to-thirty-somethings to find peer community and build lasting relationships. Today, over four thousand active members gather bimonthly at more than four hundred local tables in over one hundred cities and towns worldwide (The Dinner Party).

Finding community is a key part of their recovery. Whether it be groups like the Dinner Party or amongst family and friends, building camaraderie with those who "get it" can be immensely powerful. And while a pandemic certainly makes in-person gatherings challenging, I've found that even joining Facebook groups designed for women like me struggling with infertility have given me a safe, understanding space.

Beyond how belonging makes us feel, there are also larger health and wellness repercussions at play. Social psychologist and Stanford assistant professor Gregory Walton conducted a "belong intervention," which studies participants who are going through a difficult period. The belonging intervention uses a technique known as "attributional retraining" to help people shift blame for negative events from "It's just me" to "I'm not alone, and there are others going through it."

"Belonging is a psychological lever that has broad consequences," writes Walton. "Our interests, motivation, health and happiness are inextricably tied to the feeling that we belong to a greater community that may share common interests and aspirations... Isolation, loneliness and low social status can harm a person's subjective sense of well-being, as well as his or her intellectual achievement, immune function and health. Research shows that even a single instance of exclusion can undermine well-being, IQ test performance and self-control." (Enayati 2012).

This could explain why so many 9/11 Surviving Children have found comfort in community. It explains why I also have gravitated towards those who are also struggling with infertility. While I love my family and friends dearly and know that they mean well, they don't understand what I'm going through. There are others out there like me who know what it's like to walk this journey. If there is something to be learned from this research and the experience of 9/11 Surviving Children, it's that we are not meant to carry our grief alone.

THE PRESENT

—

When I first met Jon, I was completely oblivious to the challenges he had encountered in his childhood. I believe this is how many relationships start, just barely scratching the surface of who the other person is. Once trust is established, you can begin to peel back the layers that make up a lifetime. When we learn what happened to them, we can begin to better understand their responses and behaviors. When Jon first shared his 9/11 story with me in the Bonefish Grill restaurant so many years ago, I couldn't believe this had happened to someone like him. His optimism, resilience, and kindness seemed to negate everything I thought I knew about trauma.

By peeling back the layers in each interview, I now understand how Jon can be who he is and still have had this horrible event happen to him. I understand it because I've seen how other 9/11 Surviving Children also managed it. Even still, the resiliency I see in them is nothing short of a miracle. There are so many times where they could've been shut out from the light if it hadn't been for the support they received in multiple areas of their lives. It's easy to see what could have gone wrong, and yet the stars seemed to align for their healing.

Today, many of them are leading full lives *because* of the skills they acquired towards resiliency throughout the past several years. They faced countless setbacks head on and still kept trudging on. After a tough journey, we imagine they might look like weary travelers, too exhausted to lift their heads. Yet, the opposite couldn't be truer. We now get to see the fruits of their labor. It's an exciting opportunity for a "where are they now" reflection on this fascinating group of people.

For those of us still walking in the middle of our grief and trauma, showing the success that many 9/11 Surviving Children are experiencing today is a beacon of hope. It's a reminder that we are not our circumstances, and that this time is just a season. A new season of growth and prosperity is just around the corner.

PETE DAVIDSON

Many know of Pete Davidson, but don't know his full story. Having started his comedy career at such a young age, Davidson has grown up in the public eye. It's incredible to think of all he has accomplished in his twenty-seven years of life. As one of the youngest cast members to ever join SNL, he has been bringing his dark humor to the show for the past six years. Whether it be his SNL fame or his tragedy that brought him into the spotlight, Pete's personal life has always been at the forefront. From his failed engagement with Ariana Grande to his battles with drugs and depression, fans and media alike are always looking to learn more.

In 2020, Pete released his most recent project—a film called *The King of Staten Island*. The movie provided a therapeutic way for Pete to allow the outside world in and communicate what he's been feeling since the loss of his dad.

The film follows Scott Carlin—played by Pete—after losing his dad, Stan, in the "Paramount Hotel Fire" building collapse. Much of the trauma that his character Scott experiences mirrors the real-life experiences that Pete went through.

"When you become fodder for tabloids, you don't really have a say in how you're perceived or the truth or any of that, for that matter," says Pete. "So I really took advantage of this opportunity to show how I truly feel. And I think that there's something beautiful in that." (Edgers 2020).

It is hard to deny that Pete has done something beautiful with his grief. For Pete, his sense of humor can be directly attributed to his tumultuous childhood and loss of his father. Some of his jokes about 9/11 are so crass they make you question if you should laugh or not.

Nowhere was Pete's use of his tragedy as humor more blatant than during a *Comedy Central Roast* episode on Justin Bieber that aired in 2015. When it was his turn, Davidson said he used to be sad he grew up without his dad, but after meeting Bieber's father, he's grateful he is dead. Without skipping a beat, he then turned to Snoop Dogg and Kevin Hart and said, "*Soul Plane* was the worst experience of my life involving a plane."

Whether used as a mask from the pain or as a healthy coping mechanism, we cannot deny that Pete has been extremely successful in his comedic endeavors. The world is watching Pete's next steps, as his opportunity and potential for the future are truly limitless.

MARIA GARCIA

For Maria Garcia, now thirty years old, her love of the arts and passion to help other kids like her inspired her career path. In 2017, Maria received her master's degree in Mental Health Counseling with a specialization in Expressive Arts Therapy. She uses many of the same techniques and practices that she found helpful as a child for the kids she works with.

Maria feels grateful that she is able to give back in this way. She's seen how people have rallied behind her in her own life, and recognizes that she can now make a difference in the lives of others.

Maria is driven to helping children who are less fortunate. The passion is clear and evident in her voice while she shares the great need that is in the communities she serves.

Many of the kids Maria works with remind her of herself. Because of her experiences, Maria finds herself to be more empathetic and willing to put herself in others' shoes.

"I'm very mindful about all of the things surrounding a person, as I am with the kids that I'm working with. There's so many things that are interconnected that are not working for each child. I get to help them figure out which things are going to help them move in a direction to address both the behavioral and emotional problems."

Maria recalls having the same empathy returned to her when she was a child and how that was crucial for her development. Encountering people who were willing to see her as a whole person helped her to get to the root of why she was acting out. Her mom was one of those advocates who acknowledged the circumstances that drove Maria's behavior. On days where Maria would run and hide, her mom was always there and provided her with the resources she needed to work through her challenges. Not everyone could see past Maria's behavioral issues. From teachers who were not supportive or empathetic to peers who couldn't understand her pain—Maria began to question who her inner circle would be.

While this questioning left Maria in a place of uncertainty, it ultimately led her to find her truest passions and her tribe of people, who respect and value her for who she is.

THE THOMAS SISTERS

Mary Thomas, now twenty-seven, knows that her actions are influenced by the loss of her dad. She recalls countless vacations where her dad had the video camera in hand, documenting every moment of those precious days. Because of the love she felt from her dad as a parent, Mary looks forward to the day she has her own children. After postponing her wedding due to the pandemic, Mary recently married her boyfriend of eleven years. Mary dreams of trips to Disney and quality time spent with her future family. She looks for ways to keep her dad's memory alive, hoping to name her kids after him.

Mary's hope for a family is rooted in the family man her dad was. She looks for ways to keep his memory alive by finding ways she and her community can continue to recognize his sacrifice as a firefighter on 9/11.

"They give out a Patriot Award at my dad's high school every year, and I sit on the selection committee. We always say that our dad was our hero first, and I'm glad I get to honor him still today in these ways."

Bridget is twenty-four, and her reach and advocacy now extend to children in need.

"I currently work in a special needs school with my mom and am getting my masters in social work. I want to help kids like me who had it rough. I know that will make my dad proud."

For Bridget, it's about helping others the way her dad did. While her job doesn't send her running into burning buildings, she sees the work she does as just as important. In many ways, the support she provides these special needs children with can be lifesaving. By teaching them the skills to successfully manage the challenges they've been given, Bridget is equipping them to have a brighter future.

Their sister Rose, now twenty-two, is training to become a dog groomer. Rose takes after her dad with her kind and compassionate heart. She loves and cares for animals more than anything in the world. Despite her challenges with porphyria, she finds ways to persevere, stay active, and keep her body moving.

The girls love to visit Disney together as it's truly their "happy place." As the world shifts to a post-pandemic world, they look forward to revisiting and spending many more magical moments there together.

NICOLE FOSTER

Rose isn't the only one overcoming her physical limitations. Today, Nicole Foster is cancer-free. She continues to seek treatment and therapy for her generalized anxiety disorder, something she feels is a lifelong process of healing for her.

"I think this year I've experienced more grief over losing my dad, which was unexpected. I think everything's been unexpected this year with the COVID-19 pandemic, and so I'm working through that as well."

In 2020, Nicole graduated from Columbia with a master's degree in Psychology and Spirituality Mind Body studies. She is now a board-certified Health and Wellness Coach, helping her clients reduce stress and optimize their well-being. The job seems to be a perfect fit as her own experiences with tragedy, grief, and trauma remind her of how important wellness can be to overall recovery.

"I'm really focused and passionate about well-being as these practices helped me through my own struggles."

As if Nicole weren't busy enough, she is also coauthoring a book with a family friend—Donna Gaffney—who is a nurse psychotherapist that is very involved in supporting the 9/11 community. The pair are writing a book for nurses on how they can improve their well-being through evidence-based strategies and solutions. The book comes at a time where the healthcare industry is under much duress from the impacts of the COVID-19 pandemic.

"Especially this year, we really found that there's a need for that healthcare space. We're hoping to give back in that way."

The empathy that Nicole has grown into after losing her dad has inspired the work she does to help others. Even still, it can be challenging to forgive those who made these events happen. With so many charged opinions out there around 9/11, it is easy to see why Nicole may struggle with finding her unique voice on the subject. Overall, Nicole is still hurting from the loss and recognizes her journey has been anything but linear.

Nicole's biggest internal struggle is related to her stance on terrorism. As she looks for ways to let go and forgive in a way that is healthy, she finds there is still anger at the people who committed these acts.

"I want readers to know that families are still seeking justice and accountability for what happened regarding 9/11. The damage is still being done. Lives continue to be lost, and I'm not sure that many Americans are aware of it, at least not many outside of the NYC area."

As people who experienced two of the largest grief-filling events of our century, how do the 9/11 Surviving Children face the challenges of the world, and what do they think these times call for? While there continue to be challenges for the 9/11 Surviving Children, Nicole Foster reminds us that there is also a lot to celebrate.

"Although there's so much pain and suffering of these families, there's also a lot of love and light pouring on each of us. Lots of us lost parents that day, and we're trying to make the world a better place than it was on the worst day of our lives. So, I think that will always be my mission, and thousands of other kids' missions."

MATTHEW BOCCHI

There are so many moments in my chat with Matthew Bocchi where I couldn't believe we were "going there" in our conversation. As soon as I thought a question had gone too far, Matthew continued to be open and vulnerable. As we uncovered the deepest, darkest parts of his experiences, twenty-nine-year-old Matthew and I were able to open the door and have a similar chat on his stance on terrorism.

For Matthew, it comes down to recognizing that there are good people and bad people and all in-between—no matter where they are from and what they believe.

Matthew compared this to the Black Lives Matter movement and police brutality. With social unrest at an all-time high, we currently find ourselves questioning the systems that allow for the black community to suffer exponentially over their white peers. Matthew mentions how there are cops in his life who he loves and are incredible people, while the world seems to be painting all cops as bad. He feels that in this same way, there are Muslims who would never do anything like what the hate groups that carried out 9/11 did. To someone not personally impacted by 9/11, this might seem like a basic lesson in empathy. For someone whose father was murdered by terrorists, it's a huge step.

As he finds peace in his sobriety, his call to action is for everyone to love others and stop looking for someone to blame. Only then can we begin to uncover the real challenges that plague us.

Matthew recognizes that even with all the incredible work he's done in AA and other outlets, every day is still not perfect. There are days where he is ready to return to the rabbit hole of photos and video footage from 9/11. With his book *Sway* now published, he looks forward to being able to continue to share his message with the world, particularly in schools where he can help young people recognize that there is always a way out.

THE BURNETT SISTERS

The Burnett sisters are living and leading full lives as they begin entering the workforce. They've all seen great success in their academic careers.

Following in their father's footsteps, Halley and Anna Clare attended Pepperdine University. Twins Halley and Madison are now twenty-five years old have both obtained their master's degrees. Their sister, Anna Clare, is now twenty-three years old. If you didn't know their tumultuous past, it would seem as if the Burnett sisters have easily floated through life, with everything always working out in their favor. Behind the scenes, the lessons of hard work and determination they learned from their parents have guided them through every step.

Halley laughs when she thinks about the similarities between her and her father, and how that has come to play in her own career. Beyond attending the same school, Halley loves numbers and is very career oriented, just like him. At the time of his death, Halley's dad Thomas was vice-president and COO of Thoratec, a medical device company. As he was a major leader in the company, his career required him to be analytical and driven; something Halley carries with her today. She recently landed a job as a financial analyst in commercial real estate.

Beyond starting their careers, the sisters continue to give back to their communities in memory of their father. Through their work with the Tom Burnett Family Foundation, the family has educated thousands of children about the importance of citizenship and leadership.

Their father's last words to their mother were, "We're going to do something." The Burnett family encourages others to be active in their communities and stand up for what they believe in. This mantra has become the North Star that guides the way for all their endeavors.

As the Burnett's reflect on the turmoil our nation is in today, there is a sadness and grief that weigh on her family. Halley worries that her dad and the others on Flight 93 will have died for nothing if America continues its current streak of divisiveness and disinterest in solving our challenges together. When Halley hears sentiments from folks that they'd like to leave the country—or that don't want to help to make it better—she feels that people are forgetting all of the things Tom Burnett fought for that day. While we don't know exactly where the plane was headed, we do know that the passengers of Flight 93 saved the lives of many of our nation's leaders that day with their valiant efforts.

Halley recalls that our American-ness is what brought us together after 9/11. We put differences aside to work towards a common goal. But as we see politicians continue to name call and make personal attacks on others, it seems impossible to imagine how we might have a healthy conversation around change.

Halley believes that a victim mentality may be at the root of many of our nation's problems. Our country and our people can't always be the moral good guy and never at fault. We act surprised when other nations want to attack us instead of looking at the cause and effect that led us to these moments. And yet, Halley and her family, who had every right to act the victim, never presented themselves as such.

"We are victors, not victims. We rose above our circumstances, and we are better for it."

ANNE NELSON

Anne Nelson's story is proof that people can live through not one but multiple traumas and still recover. The death of Anne's sister was a wake-up call on many fronts. Today, Anne is thirty-one years old and tries to honor her sister and dad in all that she does.

Anne's sister, Caitlin, was a fervent supporter of organ donation. When she died, she donated her heart, lungs, kidney, pancreas, and bone and tissue grafts. Anne speaks at local schools and churches about the importance of organ donation in her sister's memory.

"I am also the captain of a 5K team for New Jersey Sharing Network which is involved in organ and tissue donation, and one year we were the top fundraising team at the event."

Even with these incredible accomplishments under her belt, Anne and her community are still doing more to keep her sister and dad's memories alive. Anne is now a special needs teacher at an elementary school, a career choice that she believes honors both of her loved ones.

Right before 9/11, Anne's dad was enrolled in Seton Hall University. He was going to graduate school there to further his law enforcement career. Education was important to him, and he wanted to learn as much as he could so that he could share his knowledge with his recruits.

Anne's sister, Caitlin, was also driven to make a difference in her career. She was a Social Work major and was interning at an inner-city school before she passed. Caitlin was passionate about giving back to the children in those communities, a trait that inspired Anne as she became a teacher.

"I take a little bit of both of them in what I'm doing and I try to carry them with me through that."

Anne feels that she has found a different perspective on life with new opportunities. She tends to regularly engage in random acts of kindness in the memory of her father and sister.

"I'm more open to novel things. I also try to identify something positive about each day. Beginning each morning with contemplating what I'm thankful for on that day is a process that is tremendously gratifying for me."

Finding something to be grateful for hasn't always come easily for Anne. Losing both her father and her sister led to many questions about why these things were happening to her. It has taken a lot of soul searching, but realizing that she has no choice but to get up and keep moving forward has changed her perspective. In a sentiment similar to the one provided by fellow 9/11 Surviving Child, Halley Burnett, Anne believes that continuing to act like a victim turns us into a shell of the person we truly are.

"The only way out of playing the victim card is forgiveness. Once I was able to let go and forgive whatever events allowed me to lose two people I loved, I started to see bits and pieces of myself coming back as I shed away the hurt and anger I was holding on to."

JON LYNCH

People often ask, "What's different about that guy?" in regard to my husband, Jon. Even I have asked the question. "How can he be so loving and compassionate when he has had such horrible things happen to him?"

At thirty-three years old, my husband Jon is the most compassionate and thoughtful person I know. He constantly puts others first. He is always first to raise his hand to help. He knows where to step in before people even ask. When I wanted to leave my full-time, salaried job for a six-month internship one thousand miles from home, he cheered me along every step. When I wanted to pursue my MBA, he picked up the extra housework so I could study. When I wanted to write a book about his life and experiences, he opened up his heart to me in ways I could never imagine. If all my gushing hasn't proven it to you, he is an all-around lovable and likable guy and a friend to many.

In his typical fashion, Jon continued to make lemonade from lemons after being laid off. In 2020, thirty-two thousand workers were laid off from Disney due to the pandemic, and he was one of them (Low 2021). He started his own business as a craftsman, and found so many rallying behind him and others who were out of work in the Central Florida area. And, after 412 days of being out of work (but who's counting), Jon was called back to work for the Walt Disney Company, where he is a Jungle Cruise Skipper until Entertainment is ready to welcome him back. He credits his faith and perseverance for getting him through the toughest times.

"My faith reminds me that there is a better, eternal life promised. I also know that being kind is the best way to prevent something like 9/11 from happening ever again. Kindness is contagious."

In a pandemic-ridden world, "contagious" is a word met with trepidation. However challenging it may seem right now, you can still spread kindness without spreading germs. We live more interconnected than ever, and yet people are at their loneliest. Imagine how the tiniest bit of kindness—a "just checking in" phone call or an encouraging word on a timeline—can change someone's world.

MARK LYNCH

Jon's brother Mark Lynch is now twenty-one years old and excited about starting his career. Mark tries to emulate the helping mentality that his dad exhibited. From running in to save others on 9/11 and always lending a helping hand, their dad left a legacy that Mark seeks to continue. Mark carries that torch forward as he is currently completing a five-year undergrad-into-master's program to become a special education teacher.

"I've been volunteering with special needs kids for a long time and I know that my dad's legacy inspired me to do that and helped me find this career path."

Mark is also a part of a STEM program at his school, which he credits to his dad's interest in engineering and technology. What Mark finds most fascinating is how many common interests he shares with a dad he doesn't remember. The lessons he has learned and their shared DNA leave the legacy of his father ingrained in Mark today.

Even though Mark doesn't remember the camaraderie amongst Americans that followed 9/11 himself, he has often heard of the united front we seemed to have. He is discouraged that Americans haven't taken a similar stance during COVID-19.

"After 9/11, there was no one who said that 9/11 was a good thing that happened. Where everyone stood was clear, and we all mourned the loss. I just can't understand why we wouldn't have the same outlook now, especially when there are days where more people die from COVID-19 in a day than died in 9/11."

Still, Mark is hopeful that his generation is full of change-makers who can flip the script on the divisiveness of our time. He pours this energy and hope into the students he mentors every day.

REBECCA ASARO

As a first responder, thirty-year-old Rebecca is one of the first people we run to in the time of crises. Rebecca is living up to her dad's legacy, taking care of others and not taking any day for granted. Even while she surrounds herself with other first responders who are doing so much good in the world, she worries that something has changed about the hearts of people, but maybe not for the better.

"America as a whole is becoming complacent and numb to tragedy. During this COVID-19 pandemic, I've heard so many relate what they're feeling now to the same fear and uncertainty that they had after 9/11."

And yet, the comparison of 9/11 to COVID-19 is one that doesn't sit well with Rebecca. As the death toll rose for COVID-19 and surpassed the count for deaths on 9/11, the commentary from the peanut gallery has been less than appreciated.

As a firefighter, Rebecca is well-positioned to greatly influence the community she touches. Rebecca does not take this opportunity for granted, which was made clear during the ceremony where both she and her brother became firefighters. Every news station wanted a story that day about the two 9/11 Surviving Children who followed in their dad's footsteps. Rebecca remained stoic and gracious, answering the myriad of questions with great care. For her, this was an opportunity to shine a light on others. The servant heart that led her to this career is the very same that allows her to openly share her experiences with others in hopes of helping them walk through their own challenges.

CAT BRENNAN

Cat Brennan, now twenty years old, has a lot to share on why she feels the pandemic situation resulting from COVID-19 is different than 9/11.

On 9/11, the image of the Twin Towers billowing smoke was burned into all of our brains. Today's burned-in image is a mask, which doesn't seem to hold the same weight. Is it that we are overstimulated in an endless-scroll world, combined with desensitization from a world that reacts to tragedy with complacency? Today, there does not seem to be the same camaraderie and optimism that we had as a nation post–9/11. Maybe it's that the human brain just can't process all of the hurt and pain we've suffered collectively this year, so it chooses to ignore it. Either way, Cat has some thoughts on how we can move forward together.

"In my family, we always say to live every day like it's 9/12. On 9/12 we were united. We took nothing for granted. We put our differences aside and supported each other."

There are many times during these interviews where I've shaken my head in disbelief. Sometimes the disbelief comes from a place of total horror at the recollection of these experiences. Other times it's from a place of total awe and admiration for the interviewee. This sentiment was one of those total awe and admiration moments, given how painful that day must have been for Cat, her eight-months-pregnant mom, and their surrounding family. It's an example of the beacon of hope and love that Cat's family experienced and hopes to share out with the rest of the world.

PRESENT TENSE

While I hoped that the Surviving Children I spoke to would be experiencing the same growth and fullness of life that Jon has, I have to say I was initially worried about what I'd find. I prayed that Jon's resilience wouldn't be an anomaly, and I was pleasantly surprised by the overall success of those I had the opportunity to speak with.

If we define "success" as living a healthy, full life, equipped with the tools to handle life's challenges, then this group is far exceeding expectations. Not every 9/11 Surviving Child is a famous comedian or a WWE star. And yet, there's something to be said for the way this incredible group of people is making immense strides in their communities.

THE PRESENT IS A GIFT

———

What 9/11 Surviving Children share on these pages encourages me to continue questioning my own life experiences and opportunities for growth. Their ability to see the present day as what it is—a gift—has inspired my own transformation.

Sure, 9/11 Surviving Children's circumstances are certainly extraordinary, but the skills to overcome our challenges are not. We all have the power within us to rise up and move beyond our challenges.

BOUNDARIES

As I've become more vocal about our struggle in having a child, I have learned that there are safe spaces and not-so-safe spaces for me to share. People I thought would be supportive were not emotionally available to hear my pain. I had to evaluate whether these relationships were life-giving for me. If I found that they were not, I stepped back from those relationships. Distancing myself from those who wouldn't allow me to sit in my pain was a painful process, but it helped me to find others who were ready to be there for me.

Our therapist recommended a rating scale for our relationships, with a five being life-giving and a one being life-sucking. Doing these exercises helped me see that I had some twos in my life—relationships where I left drained and deflated after every conversation. Now, I recognize that not every relationship I have is going to be a perfect five all the time. Where I can, I want to surround myself with people who lift me up rather than put me down. Setting boundaries on how much time I give my three, two, and one relationships has given me immense freedom and peace.

Professionals seem to agree with the benefits of this type of boundary setting. According to Mariana Bockarova, a psychology researcher at the University of Toronto, boundaries are what we are willing or not willing to say along with what we are willing or not willing to let in (Eckel 2019). As we live in the age of self-expression, and as social media gives us the ability to welcome thousands of people into our homes and minds, the concept of boundaries can become blurry. Being clear about what you're willing to talk about and with whom is an essential part of boundary setting. When a situation makes you uncomfortable, Bockarova recommends leaving an awkward pause before answering or telling the person you care about them, but that topic is off-limits for you. (Eckel 2019). If you find that the person doesn't respond in a loving way, it may be time to reconsider your closeness with that person.

I think of how Maria learned this important lesson about boundary setting when her mom asked the 9/11 recovery team to stop contacting her if they found additional remains. Her mom has shown what it means to be an advocate for yourself. Even at the age of fifty-two, Maria's mom went back to school to receive her master's degree in Social Work, a career she now shares with her daughter. This dynamic duo exemplifies how strong parenting in the face of tragedy inspires the next generation to be more resilient than one could imagine. They know that by saying "No" and setting boundaries around certain things, they are saying "Yes" to even more.

When I started setting boundaries for myself and my relationships, I realized how much I was submitting myself to before. Rather than being an active participant in my life, I was standing by, letting whoever and whatever into my heart. Because I've said "No" to toxic relationships, I've said "Yes" to my happiness.

CIRCLE OF TRUST

Talking about infertility is still a taboo topic, but the more I share, the more in control I feel around the narrative. In some ways, it loses its power over me. Whenever I speak truth about my experiences, I hear from others who have gone through or are going through the same thing. I often wonder where these women were when I was sitting quietly in my shame and grief. If I had never spoken up, I would have never known how many others share this painful path.

Why are they silent? Why was I silent? The experience of sharing is not the same for all, and I recognize I have great privilege in my ability to be so honest on the topic. Still, for others, there is great peace in having this part of their identity tucked away. The same is true for 9/11 Surviving Children who are less public about their experiences. All of these choices are brave and honorable ones to make. The important part is that honoring yourself in whichever decision you make and recognizing that what is best for you could change over time.

For myself, I've seen how talking has changed the lives of the 9/11 Surviving Children I've spoken with. I want to change my life too. I refuse to be quiet any longer.

Being in the interview room for this book was a dynamic and colorful place to be. I could hear joy in their voices as they recalled the parents they loved so much. I could feel sadness in the painful moments of their journeys. All these emotions weaved together into a beautiful and complex tapestry of their lives.

My own story matters, too. When you're married to someone who has a story like Jon's, it can be easy to shrink into the background. Yes, I am the wife of a 9/11 Surviving Child, but that is just one part of my identity. Just like for Jon, being a 9/11 Surviving Child is just one part of his identity. And not living through the tragedy he did doesn't make my challenges or triumphs any less real or valid.

If you're reading this book and feeling like your struggles could never measure up to those of the 9/11 Surviving Children, I'm begging you to please remove those thoughts from your brains! The purpose is not to compare, but rather to find the similarities we share in our journeys. The empowerment that the 9/11 Surviving Children expressed while sharing their stories is something that really resonated with me. However, I recognize that my vulnerability has come with a *ton* of unsolicited feedback.

The comments I began to receive once opening up about our journey reminded me of when Jon and I first got married. As is to be expected in marriage, there were, and continue to be, many tough decisions for us to navigate through. Things were all hunky-dory in the honeymoon phase, that is until we started discussing whether we should move to Florida. For me, it was a resounding yes, but for Jon, who had already lived in Florida and worked for Disney years prior, the decision wasn't as clear. While I find that I've often felt empowered to make decisions on my own, Jon likes to consult the "hive mind" of those around him, especially his close family and friends. After losing his dad, the bond between him and his mom grew closer—something Jon cherishes, and I would never want to take away.

When you spend your whole life consulting others, confiding in them, and getting their opinion, it's difficult to see when it's time to step away. It's not to say that those who guided you throughout your life simply get tossed away (I wouldn't be able to survive if I never called on my parents for help when I need advice), but the relationship changes when you enter a marriage. Suddenly, you're making joint decisions within the marriage—decisions that don't all need to be run by a parent or guardian. In continuing to ask others for permission for us to move to Florida, I felt betrayed. "These are decisions we are supposed to make together!" I kept thinking.

I confided in a friend about the boundary-setting challenges I felt we were having. The last thing I wanted to do was put a wedge in between Jon and his mom, but I knew I needed something to change. My friend asked if Jon and I had established a circle of trust. We hadn't, and frankly, I had no idea what she was talking about.

She told me that the circle of trust is the circle of people who get to be key players in the big decisions in your life. The first circle should be you and your spouse only. This is your marriage and your life, so the only people who truly at the end of the day have a say should be the two of you. That doesn't mean there aren't people you consult and ask opinions of when you need help making a big decision. There are perimeter circles outside of the main circle of trust that can provide guidance but aren't necessarily a part of the decision-making process. Sometimes people in the perimeter circles aren't going to agree with all of the decisions happening inside the circle of trust—and that's okay.

Jon and I began informing others who were previously in the main circle of trust that we love them and respect their opinions and will take them into consideration when making decisions. Any advice or feedback received from perimeter circles was discussed and weighed as options within the main circle of trust. Sometimes we consult the outer circles. Sometimes we don't. Sometimes the conversation is just "We made this decision, and we hope that you support us in it."

There are some people with whom I can talk about my struggles, and then there are some others who are not in that outer circle of trust. Only a few get to know the intimate details of Jon's loss and our infertility. Even opening up about our fertility journey to that first perimeter, our parents, was something we discussed long and hard about.

I would hedge a bet and say that many 9/11 Surviving Children have developed a circle of trust even if they don't call it that. I can see it in the way they are mindful of who they share the most intimate details of their stories with. Imagine if we all were this discerning with our decision-making and storytelling. There's immense power in finding your circles. Identify those people and hold to them tightly. Remember that this is your life, and the people in it should earn the right to be a part of it.

Setting boundaries and being clear about the kind of support I need is a huge part of my story. My story is still being written. Even if I cannot choose what happens next, I can, at least, influence which characters play a leading role.

YOU ARE NOT A CAKE

"You are not a cake," my pastor said, as I feverishly took notes during the Sunday service. While I'm always happy to talk about food, I must admit I struggled to understand how I could possibly be compared to a cake, and how this message might further my development.

What my pastor was getting at is that we aren't complete yet. Maybe someday we will be a cake: perfect and warm right out of the oven. But until then, we are still being formed. Shaped. Molded into who we are and will become.

While 9/11 Surviving Children are made up of many complex ingredients, one of the most difficult to touch on was their stance on terrorism. Nicole Foster was the first besides my husband to openly share with me how she feels on the subject.

My husband also has hurt and anger in his heart towards the people who killed his father. As Christians, Jon and I believe that judgment is left up to God. Even with that belief, there is a sense of justice that he feels in his heart, along with so many questions.

As a child, it is difficult to understand why someone would do something like this. I remember my mom trying to explain 9/11 through the lens that bad people had done something to hurt us. The complexities of terrorism were lost on me as a child. Even now, as an adult, I struggle to understand what kind of world allowed so much hate to foster and grow.

I'm certain there are many things the 9/11 Surviving Children would like to ask the people who did this. Even if an eye for an eye is wanted, does it change anything? For Jon, he recognizes that the "justice" that was served —and continues to be served —against the people who made this happen doesn't bring his dad back. Seeking revenge also doesn't make the world a different place after 9/11. If anything, it just repeats the cycle of hate that got us to 9/11 in the first place.

When 9/11 happened, Americans ate up the "They hate our freedoms" sentiment faster than if we were sneaking in dessert before dinner behind our parents' backs. But if that were true, why weren't other free countries under attack? In 2004, Osama Bin Laden even responded by asking why, if this were true, had he not attacked freedom-loving Sweden? (Bergen 2006). If we took the time to learn why, could we unlock the secret to moving our nation out of victimhood?

The theories behind why and who range from outlandish (it was an inside job with the US Government at the helm) to plausible yet flawed (a response to foreign occupation). In reality, there are many factors that worked together to create the perfect storm for 9/11. Peter Bergen, co-director of the Counterterrorism and Counterinsurgency Initiative at the New America Foundation, sums it up quite eloquently:

"... 9/11 was collateral damage in a civil war within the world of political Islam. On one side there are those, like Bin Laden, who want to install Taliban-style theocracies from Indonesia to Morocco. On the other side there is a silent majority of Muslims who are prepared to deal with the west, who do not see the Taliban as a workable model for modern Islamic states, and who reject violence. Bin Laden adopted a war against "the far enemy" in order to hasten the demise of the "near enemy" regimes in the Middle East. And he used 9/11 to advance that cause. That effort has, so far, largely failed." (Bergen 2006)*

Even still, knowing that you lost a parent because it was just "collateral damage" and "wasn't personal" doesn't bring your parent back, and doubtfully makes 9/11 Surviving Children feel any better about the situation.

As I spoke with other 9/11 Surviving Children, many of them steered clear of the topic for fear of judgment around their feelings. They feel that they may be perceived as bad people if they openly talk about their anger towards the people who killed their parents.

During my time with Nicole, it was clear that she is a compassionate and thoughtful woman. When she speaks of all the heartache she's been through—from the loss of her dad to her leukemia diagnosis—she does so with grace and dignity. And, her studies on mindfulness allow her to be reflective rather than reactionary.

Compassionate and thoughtful people can still have complex emotions that fit outside of the mold we associate with those words. There is room for people to have many emotions all at the same time. Even I have to admit that there are times that I think about my sweet, loving husband and wonder how he can have so much hate in his heart for terrorists. How can he possibly be all of those things? And, if he is angry at terrorists and unforgiving of terrorists, is that okay? Does this anger make him less of a good person?

I am often quick to excuse my own shortcomings as external factors. Meanwhile, I look at others and imagine something internal is wrong with them when they act outside of their perceived persona. When we label people as kind, compassionate, or thoughtful, and they act outside of those means, we have trouble giving them grace for feeling those emotions. For example, if I'm running late, it's because traffic was awful. If someone else is running late, it's because they are irresponsible.

If my family and friends labeled me as a bad person because of all the angry outbursts I've had this year, I'd be in serious trouble. 9/11 Surviving Children, like all of us, are complex beings who are still learning and growing even twenty years later. I should give my husband—and all others—the same grace I wish people would show me in my darkest moments.

I am not a cake. I am not complete like a cake. I am still adding the necessary ingredients. I am in the oven, still baking. So are my husband and everyone else around us. They deserve the same grace that I do.

SLOW YOUR SCROLL

As a firefighter, Rebecca reminded me that for her family, their job is a daily reminder of the sacrifice her dad and many others made that day. She recognizes that people's attitudes towards tragedy have changed since the days after 9/11.

So, what is it that has changed in twenty years that took us from a place of great unity post–9/11 to a place of complacency, numbness, and division with the COVID-19 pandemic? We said, "Never Forget," but have we started to forget the lessons we learned and the kind of nation we hope to be?

As the 9/11 Surviving Children have grown up, so have we as a nation. We aren't the same United States that watched in shock and horror as the planes hit the towers. Technology alone has drastically changed since then, which has had a significant impact on the way we respond to tragedy. While we've learned a lot about many 9/11 Surviving Children that is promising, can we say the same about our nation?

Twenty years ago, we shuddered at the thought of three thousand deaths in one day. Three thousand souls: lost in an instant. It shook the United States, and the world, to its core. People were kinder, more thoughtful. We were united. But what about now? As of November 17, 2020, an average of around 918 people per day have died from COVID-19 in the US since the first case was confirmed in the country on January 20 (Elflein 2021).

Even as a self-proclaimed empath, I've felt that empathy slip away as all of the tragedy slips into the background of my newsfeed. I don't sit with anything anymore. I scroll and scroll and scroll, occasionally stopping at something of interest. I chew it up quickly and move onto the next post.

Like 9/11, it was a series of baby steps that led us to our current predicament. In the twenty years between these two major events, other events have slowly desensitized us to the plight of others. After 9/11, we were collectively grieving an immeasurable loss. We saw massive changes in legislation, regulations, and policies related to the attacks. The War on Terror began, air travel was completely transformed, and the Patriot Act allowed for increased surveillance.

And while we imagined that 9/11 was just the start of other massive foreign terrorist attacks, whether because of the policy changes or otherwise, we thankfully haven't seen something of this magnitude since 9/11. That isn't to say we haven't had our fair share of domestic terrorist activity, the Boston Marathon bombing (2013), the Charleston church shooting (2015), and the Orlando nightclub shooting (2016), to name a few. And, as soon as we thought we had put the pain of 2020 behind us, 2021 came in full force with the domestic terrorist attack on the US Capitol.

This doesn't even scratch the surface, as there have been countless non-terroristic shootings at schools, malls, and movie theaters around the country in the past twenty years. After 9/11, we were so focused on looking outside of our country for the attack that we forgot to look at ourselves. Because of it, children born in the midst of 9/11 are subject to events that have become their "normal" rather than a tragic anomaly. And yet, in all this time, despite incredible organizations such as March For Our Lives, we haven't seen any policy change related to domestic terrorism, leaving us jaded and exhausted.

Having tragedy constantly accessible from an app on your phone has its consequences. According to a study done by doctors in the International Journal of Epidemiology, the Millennial and Gen Z population is more depressed than their older counterparts (Patalay and Gage 2019). While there is a myriad of factors that could make this true, it's hard to ignore the impacts that these events and our access to them have had on their lives.

Millennial and Gen Z populations have also been the most exposed to these types of events via traditional and social media. According to research psychologist Dana Rose Garfin of UC Irvine, "People can experience collective trauma solely through the media and report symptoms that resemble those typically associated with direct trauma exposure." (Garfin 2016) Another interesting finding from the study was that people who experienced higher media exposure to an event that gave them collective trauma experience higher acute stress symptoms during subsequent events than their peers (Garfin 2016).

We've also become victims of the media age, where we can see the news play these events over and over and over until we are numb. "Another day, another mass shooting" seems to be the mantra of our people; as we shrug our shoulders and move on to the next thing in our news feeds. We scroll, scroll, and scroll some more. These factors may have led to the desensitization and complacency that Rebecca Asaro recognizes. After a year of watching COVID-19 wreak havoc on our world, we are numb to the news cycle and the deaths.

This isn't to say that we should live each day in a constant state of fear. We should, instead, be more thoughtful of how much time we spend on media platforms and make changes that demonstrate our empathy towards others. If we spent less time glued to our phones, we might be more able to use our time and resources to make sure that events like this can never happen again. And even if not, imagine what we could do with this incredible technology at our disposal, pivoting away from emotionally toxic material and using the tool to become more informed and active.

I've started to change some of my tech habits, which has helped me to sit and reflect more. Phones no longer come into our bedroom at night—they are plugged in in the bathroom. Jon and I both have timers set on our social media apps. We swapped passwords for the timer so that we cannot unlock the apps after fifteen minutes of usage ourselves. Doing so has made me more intentional about my time on social media and limited my trauma exposure. Slowing my scroll has made me less anxious and stressed and more able to hold real, authentic, and empathetic conversations.

NEVER FORGET

We have a permanent "ofrenda" for Jon's dad in our house. If you aren't familiar, an "ofrenda" is an altar celebrating your loved ones that is traditionally a part of the Dia de los Muertos celebration in Mexico. Here we display pictures of Jon's dad along with memorabilia he has acquired over the years: the sign for the street in Staten Island that was named after his dad, a piece of the World Trade Center steel, the program from the White House Lawn when they received his dad's Medal of Valor. The ofrenda is our way of never forgetting.

There are countless events that have changed the course of history: World War I, World War II, 9/11, and the COVID-19 pandemic, to name a few. Others were more positive: the Renaissance, the invention of the printing press, man landing on the moon, the Fall of the Berlin Wall. History has shown us that these events never stop. All we can do is be more prepared for them.

September 11 itself has become so many things. Despite the unity it created, it also became a political football. For better or for worse, 9/11 has been tossed around in the mouths of politicians for years, implementing many policies as a result. While there are many reasons that contribute to this being the case, the most devastating result is that real people and their families are subjected to the death of their loved ones being used to push an agenda. We see this playing out in real time as the COVID-19 pandemic becomes an opportunity for politicians to score points based on how they handle it.

It would be naïve to say that other events through history that involved death were responded to with bipartisanship. Even with the political undertones that fueled 9/11 and post–9/11 policy, for the most part, leaders from both parties set aside their differences, united behind a national strategy, and held each other accountable to implement it. What has polarized us so much in the past twenty years that we cannot do the same to combat the COVID-19 virus?

Here we are arguably more divided than ever. In the face of another national (and international) tragedy, we have division and hate in a way we've never seen before. The powers that be made COVID-19 political when it didn't have to be.

Like 9/11, we have an opportunity to put ourselves aside and put the collective well-being ahead of personal interest.

My husband lost so much in 9/11. *We* lost so much in the past year. I've lost myself.

When we vowed to "Never Forget," we also promised to never forget how we stood by each other that day. We promised to never forget how three thousand people did not wake up on 9/12, and yet in some ways, we did. We had a chance to live while they didn't. We had an opportunity to take care of the spouses and children who were left behind. The resilient 9/11 Surviving Children didn't become that way by accident. It took years of nurturing, guidance, and support from their communities.

I haven't been very grateful, gracious, or kind recently. Sometimes even I, a wife of a 9/11 Surviving Child, forget. I've started to ignore the little whispers throughout the day to text a friend in need or send a card in the mail just because. While the ofrenda remains as a gentle reminder, I've gotten out of practice. Rather than jumping into action, the pain and sadness of the pandemic and our pregnancy journey have left me desensitized. It took having these interviews for me to say, "No more." When my spirit says "Act," I can no longer ignore it. I cannot forget how I have felt when in that dark place, thinking I'm alone. When I finally looked up and realized how loved I am, I recognized I didn't want to go one more day without letting others know that the same is true for them.

Bringing attention to the camaraderie that 9/11 Surviving Children felt on 9/12 is not meant to discount the experiences of those who didn't feel that camaraderie. Unfortunately, the warmth and care that 9/11 families experienced weren't a reality for everyone. White Americans found camaraderie, but those who were or were perceived to be Muslim found themselves subject to threats and violent actions. It only felt nice in the in-group—the out-group saw the worst of us. As 9/11 became a symbol of American patriotism, Muslims both mourned the tragedy of 9/11 and became outcasts of the "other" all at once.

Due to the nature of how interviews were carefully conducted only with those who felt comfortable sharing their stories, I did not have the opportunity to speak with any 9/11 Surviving Children who are Muslim. And yet, I recognize that this is a significant and underrepresented part of the narrative.

The horrors this group of people endured—including but not limited to the loss of a parent and the ostracizing of their people—is something I cannot fathom. Even still, we see this blame behavior continue as we witness rampant xenophobia in the face of the COVID-19 pandemic.

What drives the constant need to compare and blame? Is it our way of making sense of what we cannot understand? In doing so, are we aware of how harmful these thought patterns can be to those directly impacted?

In the midst of COVID-19. In the middle of my infertility. In the memory of 9/11. We still have that opportunity to make the world a better place. We have a chance to live for all of those who did not have a 9/12, and to care for the people impacted by this virus.

As painful as our path to baby Lynch has been and continues to be, I hope that I never forget how this felt. When the blessing is finally here and the pain of waiting is long gone, I hope the lessons come with me. The patience and love I received from others and gave myself are things I never want to lose.

Every day my baby is not yet here is a day I don't get to love on them. Every day Jon's father is not with us is a stolen opportunity. We have a duty to be grateful, gracious, and kind—because others would give anything to have one more day with their loved ones.

COURAGE

People often tell my husband and me that we have so much "courage" for sharing our stories. Whether it be our walk with infertility or the loss of his dad, we are nothing if not an open book. I've never thought of this as courageous until people started mentioning it. To me, being courageous was reserved for first responders, military, and the like. How could our vulnerability possibly be associated with that?

The dictionary definition of courage is "the quality of mind or spirit that enables a person to face difficulty, danger, pain, etc., without fear" (Dictionary.com). While I wouldn't say we share our stories without fear, it has definitely been difficult and painful. Peeling back the facade that "everything is fine" and showing our true, vulnerable selves has often left us feeling naked and bare. But the more we share, the more comfortable it becomes.

According to Bill George, "Courage is neither an intellectual quality, nor can it be taught in the classroom. It can only be gained through multiple experiences involving personal risk-taking." (George 2017)

Surviving Children have certainly done their fair share of personal risk-taking, but it's likely that you have as well. When you lose someone or something closer to you, the experience tends to bring things into perspective. As I've learned from the countless interviews in this book, one's purpose for living becomes clearer after tragedy: to honor the memory of a loved one, to live every day to the fullest, to make sure that something like this never happens again. These sentiments become like principles and provide a guide when faced with the next tough decision. When you've already lost it all, what more do you have to lose by taking a calculated risk?

When we step out in faith, we become victors over our circumstances. If there is anything that the 9/11 Surviving Children have taught me, it's that we cannot allow what happens to us to define us. In addition, no amount of trying to shield or protect ourselves and our children will change the fact that bad things happen. When we do so, we actually do a disservice for when they become adults and are unable to cope with anything that does not go their way. That isn't to say every child should have a life-altering tragedy early on, but that a healthy dose of reality can better prepare all of us for what lies ahead and what we are capable of.

You already have what it takes. You just need to unleash the courage within you. If every single person reading this book were to apply the learnings on courage we've gained from the 9/11 Surviving Children, there's no telling the impact we could make in our communities and families.

THE FUTURE

——

The 9/11 Surviving Children are coming of age in a turbulent time, but they won't be shaken. They are rooted in the legacy their parents left behind and determined to make the world a better place, despite the challenges we face. I am grateful that the 9/11 Surviving Children are our future voters, teachers, and doctors.

In this chapter, we share the hopes and dreams 9/11 Surviving Children have of the future. Not only for themselves, but for the world. We talk about what they'd like to see from our leaders moving forward and how we as humans can better care for one another. What they bring to the table isn't just a blind optimism, but a burning desire to impact change.

Here we have an opportunity to step into their shoes and help to create the kind of world and environment they are looking to foster. May their outlooks be the call to action we need to be active participants and help make this future a reality.

JON LYNCH

For my husband, it's hard to say what the future holds. Two years ago, it was all very clear. We would continue working in our dream jobs until retirement. Keep traveling the world. We'd have a family, two kids or so. It was all set up to be a very exciting time—until it wasn't.

Certainly, being called back to work has brought some things back into focus for us; however, we are hesitant to get too comfortable. We've seen how our world can be flipped upside down in an instant. Stability is an illusion. What I do know is that Jon will continuously look for ways to serve others.

I'd love to say that Jon's future also holds serving as a father. I know that he will be a great one. He will love his kids so much—he already does. He will bring a compassion to fatherhood that only someone who experienced a great loss like his could bring.

There are days where it feels like it will never happen. I finally know, with every fiber of my being, that it will. While it continues to be something I want so badly, surrendering it all to God and his timing has changed my perspective. While I look forward to being the mother of these future children, I am overjoyed at the thought of Jon being a dad. They will benefit so greatly by having Jon as their father, and I can only imagine the kind, compassionate people they will become because of him.

The peace and love that Jon radiates through all circumstances continue to be his guiding posts through the storms. It's this energy that permeates his relationships and impacts all who know him. It's how I know that no matter what our future holds, we will be okay.

MARIA GARCIA

In Maria Garcia's work, she is actively involved in raising the next generation. She is excited by what she's seen in them: a recognition that the landscape right now is complicated but that there is still an opportunity to change things. She says by what she's seen—the future looks bright.

Most notably, Maria sees how the children she works with are deeply involved and interested in politics. They see the super polarization happening in the United States and want to correct it.

Maria shares, "There was once a time where being a Republican or a Democrat didn't necessarily mean you were viewed as a good or bad person, but we've become so polarized. Most people are somewhere in the middle. Both parties are not doing the United States justice and we are left to fend for ourselves."

However, the kids Maria works with are ready to take a stand. While this is just a small sampling of the up-and-coming generation, the idea still excites me. They are the politicians of the future, and they seem a lot more levelheaded than what we've got now. They understand there are complexities of everything that we're going through and that while nothing is as black and white as it seems, we've got to start working together, on both sides of the political spectrum, in order to make a difference.

"The teenagers I work with tell me they cannot wait until they're eighteen and can vote. Even for the 2020 election, they were getting involved in all of these drives and were calling and posting on Twitter to spread the message that they want people to get out there and vote. Right now, it feels so messy and so many politicians don't genuinely care. I do wonder if there were to be another national tragedy like 9/11 how they would respond."

Maria thinks we are seeing exactly how they would respond as we deal with the political repercussions of the COVID-19 pandemic, and it isn't pretty.

"During 9/11, politicians found someone to place the blame on. With COVID-19, we have no one to blame but ourselves. And yet, we've found a way to pin it on a group of people, which has led to the heartbreaking acts of xenophobia happening throughout the country."

As our nation's leaders and the people we trust with our news and information lead us astray, we are left wondering what it means to lead in a crisis. Whether great leaders are made from crises, or they simply rise up and show their true strengths because of it, it's no secret that tragedy often brings triumph in this way. While our political leaders haven't exactly been the heroes we all wanted and needed, we must look to others and to the 9/11 Surviving Children for guidance on what the future of leadership looks like.

ANNE NELSON

Anne Nelson recognizes that it isn't always easy to live her life, but that doing so is a testimony to others.

"Sometimes people ask me, 'How are you doing it?' And a lot of times I think there is no other choice. I make the choice every morning to get out of bed and put my best foot forward. I have the courage to face anything that comes."

The courage that Anne finds in herself each day plays an essential role in the success of the 9/11 Surviving Children I spoke to; it's an incredible trait to have to live and lead with. As Anne took on the role of teacher, these traits empower her to encourage vulnerability in her classrooms. Even when Anne is struggling herself, she finds that courage within her to make space for the needs of her students. When a student is struggling, Anne is quick to recognize it. By speaking about her own challenges, she shows her students they have a safe space to be transparent as well.

By investing in the children she works with, Anne is investing in the future. When she gets out of bed and puts her best foot forward, she does it for them. She knows those kids need her, and her experiences help to make her a source of comfort for them.

MARK LYNCH

Mark Lynch is uniquely positioned at an age where his life is so directly impacted by an event he doesn't remember. He and his experiences are shaped by the timing of both 9/11 and COVID-19, as he now looks to the future for hope. If there is anything he finds that he is grateful for as he has been impacted by these events, it is the resilience, understanding, and compassion he has gained.

These are the traits that he feels will make those who experience grief and trauma stand out from the rest. They are the traits of incredible leaders, something I believe Mark already is as he pursues his career in special education.

Because of that understanding, Mark embraces and leads others free of judgment. I remember the first time Mark told me he was considering a career in special education. After seeing his involvement in this community throughout high school, I knew it was a perfect fit. I've seen Mark pour such love into this community, from involving himself in the Partners in Learning Success (PALS) programs; to coaching special-education basketball leagues; to becoming a camp counselor at Camp PALS.

When we have empathy for others, we can understand why those around us might be responding in a certain way.

Many times, there may be something tough they are going through that is causing them to behave in that manner. When we take the time to get to know the whole person and listen to their challenges, we can often resolve many potential conflicts.

As for life advice, Mark reminds us not to sweat the small stuff. As he knows what it is to lose, he has learned how to appreciate what he has.

Mark says, "Care for the people you love and make memories with them while they are here because you never know when you might lose them." Caring is exactly what he is doing in his career and through his life as he pours into the lives of special needs children.

So often, we hear this advice, and it falls on deaf ears as we stare numbly into our smartphone screens. Mark's hope is that this sentiment encourages others to look up and live their life in the moment, providing a more present and joyful future for all.

THE BURNETT SISTERS

"I am unafraid, and I am bold," Halley Burnett told me with a fire in her eyes. These two traits are what Halley credits to her success and excitement around future endeavors.

Life begins outside of your comfort zone. Halley mentioned a sentiment from Georgia O'Keeffe that she feels says it best: "I've been absolutely terrified every moment of my life—and I've never let it keep me from doing a single thing I wanted to do." This guiding mantra may encourage you to get out of your head and start taking the steps toward boldness. People want to follow others who move confidently in the direction they want to go.

For Halley, this has meant taking a chance to live and study abroad; being one of five women in the finance major at her school; applying for jobs and schools where she didn't meet all of the qualifications—and getting offers. Case in point: when Southern Methodist University wanted several years of work experience for applicants, Halley applied anyway and was accepted. She has led with this ideal her whole life. Halley has seen success wherever she has gone because she lives unafraid and boldly.

Living and leading have helped the Burnett sisters arguably fair better than others during the pandemic. While they live with caution during this time, they hold one another closely as they recognize what they've lost before.

ALEXA EDWARDS

It wasn't until Alexa Edwards lost the ability to dance that she understood how a healthy mindset can impact the future. When Alexa suffered a broken nose and concussion, her control over things or lack thereof came swiftly into focus. The one thing she thought she had control over was now no longer an option, at least temporarily.

"I've now accepted that there are about four things I have influence over and the rest is going to happen as it will."

One of the things Alexa feels she has influence over is her social media usage—something she recognizes isn't going away anytime soon. While she may not be able to control who posts what, she can influence the amount of time she spends, the type of content she sees, and the type of content she posts herself.

"It's been easy for me to put up a front online that everything's good and not seek help. I've always taken great pride in being told that I am so happy even with everything I've been through. I've learned the best thing is to allow myself to be down when I'm down, and if I could give the future generations any advice it would be to take down the walls that social media creates to separate us and make us feel like we are never enough."

As I've thought about the "never enough" mentality that social media has personally left me with, I stand firmly by Alexa's encouragement to put less of our time and valuable attention in a platform that sometimes takes more than it can give.

MATTHEW BOCCHI

For a guy who has seen and done it all, it's easy to imagine Matthew Bocchi having a bleak outlook on the future. As we spoke about his obsession with watching 9/11 footage, he mentioned how so many people who read his book *Sway* reached out and said that they researched and watched a lot of what he had shared in the book.

Even in our interview, Matthew shared the names of videographers who captured some of the most graphic moments of 9/11 from within the towers. I had to stop myself from writing the names down. I personally had preserved myself from this type of content for a long time in an effort to protect my heart and mind.

I asked Matthew if he was bothered by people's increasing obsession to watch tragedy unfolding and how he feels this impacts the future of human relationships. I related it to the slowdown in traffic you see on the highway after an accident because everyone is rubbernecking. There seems to be this innate, morbid curiosity that keeps us coming back to watch desensitizing, violent content.

The way Matthew sees it is that it really matters *why* they are watching the content. "Are they hoping to learn more and become truly empathic to the situation? Or is there something else going on there? For my friends who reached out saying that they did more research after reading the book, I see it as their way of trying to connect with me on a level they couldn't before."

There is a healthy way for us to consume this content and remain empathic to one another. Asking ourselves critical questions after viewing is essential. What did we learn from watching this that we didn't know before? How will we treat people differently based on this new information? This type of conscious analysis may make all the difference in our relationships moving forward.

BE THE CHANGE

Although we've yet to see the full fruits of 9/11 Surviving Children's labors as they continue to mold and grow the next generation, I have no doubt that we will all benefit from their impact. They certainly are not naïve; they've seen the worst of circumstances play out in their own lives. However, they continue to maintain a hope and optimism unlike any other. It's something I hope we can all harness ourselves.

As we look to them and all those they influence to be the next leaders of our country, companies, and homes, we must remember their example and rise to meet our own challenges. We cannot rely on them to be the change alone. The lessons they've taught us are something that all of us can employ in our lives.

"Be the change" sounds like a lofty goal. But being the change doesn't have to mean grandiose gestures or donating

large sums of money. It starts with being present. Being kind.
Being vulnerable.

RISE FROM THE ASHES

——

Sometimes rising from the ashes just means acknowledging how hard things are and recognizing the sacrifices. Most of the time, just being heard is all that I need to feel understood and respected.

As I've done throughout this entire process, I have related this experience of 9/11 Surviving Children back to my fertility journey. While I would *love* if one of my family members or friends could just fix our problem, I recognize that is not the reality. Sometimes I just want them to listen and just tell me that they know it sucks but that they are here for me. As I've learned the things that I want others to say to me during my crises, I've been able to employ that amongst friends and my now fully virtual work teams. I have a better sense when they have Zoom fatigue or are frustrated by trying to make sure their child pays attention in virtual school, all while balancing their work schedule.

People tend to feel the most vulnerable when they are isolated after experiencing grief or trauma. Checking in with others is a great way to bridge the gap and let them know they are not alone.

There are so many ways in which we can rise while lifting others by putting the future dreams of 9/11 Surviving Children to work here and now.

THE REAL INFLUENCERS

"Influencer" is a term that's been tossed around frequently over the past several years. In pop culture, we often hear it in relation to social media stars who have risen to fame through their content production. These influencers typically have thousands of followers on Instagram and the like. With so many people in their sphere of "influence," brands often reach out to these people, offering them free products to promote or paying them to leave an endorsement. Their job is to encourage others to buy a product. The thought is that people who follow these accounts want to emulate them and trust their opinions, so they'll buy what they tell them to.

Prior to recent years, the term influencer was less of a job title and more of a state of being. While I cannot deny the success of social media influencers, I believe it's people like the 9/11 Surviving Children who are the true influencers of this day and age.

I see it so clearly in my husband, who has spent his life serving others, especially youth. From directing children's theatre to making kids smile while he dances down Main Street, USA, Jon has incredible influence over the communities he touches. This willingness to serve and teach others is what makes me so excited for him to be a father someday.

Several 9/11 Surviving Children are in jobs today where they have a direct influence on future generations. I don't believe this is a coincidence. Maria Garcia and Bridget Thomas are both involved in social work, leading others through their own crises. Anne Nelson and Mark Lynch have careers in special education, providing the extra level of care and support that those children need. Nicole Foster works in the health and wellness field, which couldn't be more applicable to her own trials and ability to bounce forward from them. Rebecca Asaro and four of her siblings became firefighters, which has direct influence as they put themselves in danger on a daily basis for the sake of others.

Each of them, influencers, using their own experiences to guide them. But what is it about going through tough times that makes us want to help others? Sometimes it takes knowing what that dark place feels like to recognize that no one should ever have to feel that way or need to navigate it alone. They've quite literally "been there before," helping them to empathize with those they interact with. They recognize how much they gained from the influencers in their lives: both their deceased and surviving parent, camp counselors, therapists, family, and friends. They become the influencers themselves, and because of their service, they are bound to have more real-life followers than any social media star.

Fred Rogers once said, "When I was a boy and I would see scary things in the news, my mother would say to me, '**Look for the helpers**. You will always find people who are helping.' " (Nation 2012). These helpers are the people we should be emulating.

The 9/11 Surviving Children are influencers, but they aren't superheroes. The beauty of this is that everyone, even us commoners without a cape and the ability to fly, can have influence. In fact, most of us do have influence over others—we just don't recognize it. This means we might be influencing in ways we do not intend to.

If we bring some focus to this area, what might we achieve? Sure, not all of us lost parents in 9/11, but we all have our junk. How can we use that to help others? One way might be through leading with vulnerability, which is an extremely challenging thing to do.

There are so many times I hesitated to share what we were battling through with infertility. Once I got over that hurdle and did share, I was blown away by the reception. The amount of support and stories I heard from others going through the same thing was astonishing. If you can just take that one step towards opening your heart, you could influence someone who is living through the same thing. Imagine if someone hearing your story while in the depths of their own grief is pulled out of the darkness just by knowing they aren't alone. There is no better reward in the world than knowing that you made even a small impact on someone's life.

I wanted to take stock of the ways that infertility has changed me, so I started writing down the lessons I've learned. What I found was patience, flexibility, an increased willingness to give up control, and a simple acknowledgment that things won't always go my way (which I've come to find isn't actually that simple). These are the things I hold on to and share with others in hopes of influencing in my own way. When we find the lesson in our trials, we can access our strengths and passions to seek opportunities to help others.

INTO THE UNKNOWN

If you've seen Disney's *Frozen 2*, you've most likely seen the memes that followed about Elsa's song "Into the Unknown." In this scene, Elsa is pouring her heart out, singing at the top of her lungs. It also happens to be the middle of the night. The joke is that she's waking up all of Arendelle in the process.

That's the kind of commitment I want to see in my life. Elsa doesn't care whether it was two in the morning or not. She steps unafraid and boldly into the unknown. She gives it all she's got.

It might seem silly to compare oneself to a Disney character, but the reason we love these stories so much is that we see ourselves in them. When you live unafraid and boldly, you realize that the worst thing they can say is "No." But just imagine. Imagine if they say "Yes." They can't say "Yes" if you never try.

I was getting serious Elsa vibes during my conversation with Halley Burnett. While her icy blonde hair certainly had something to do with that, it was the message she shared that resonated even more. Her encouragement to be brave and bold was one she specifically hoped would be heard by women.

This isn't because men shouldn't also live unafraid and boldly, but because for many of them it is already in their training to do so. In a world where little girls are told to be seen and not heard, living unafraid and boldly doesn't always seem like an option.

We talked about our careers, hers in finance, mine in tech, both male-dominated fields. When the only face or voice that looks and sounds like yours is your own, it can be difficult to imagine yourself in this career path. I can only imagine that the experience is even worse for our coworkers of color.

As we live in a world where women still make less than their male coworkers, Halley hopes to inspire others to reach for their dreams. According to Sheryl Sandberg, more women are advocating for themselves in terms of raises and promotions, but the gap has yet to be completely filled (Sandberg

2021). Her website, leanin.org, is an incredible resource for women looking for the tools to bravely lean in.

Halley leads by example because her dad led by example. She feels that she is unafraid and bold because of how her dad stepped into the unknown on 9/11. Because of that, Halley continues to step out of her comfort zone.

But what if you don't have a good example to follow?

As a theatre major in college, I remember several people throughout my life asking me how I became a good singer. My mom would often joke that she isn't sure because she herself doesn't have a singing bone in her body. It was clear I didn't have a good example of a singer in my home.

When I got to college, I had a voice teacher ask me what kind of music I typically listened to. I rattled off a few popular artists and band names, all of which she turned her nose up to. She advised me to "Listen to the people you want to sound like. Study them as an example."

While I didn't have an example in my own home, I had access to countless examples of well-renowned Broadway sopranos and belters.

If we could all just find one good example of someone who is living the type of life we want to have, could we believe that we could achieve it as well? Would we lean in and step out into the unknown? It's not everyone's cup of tea, but I try to do this unafraid and boldly, all while belting at the top of my lungs.

EMPATHY FIRST

Can you imagine going back to school or work after losing a loved one in 9/11? I can't. I constantly think about my husband's experience as the only one in his entire district who lost a parent that day. Not only does everyone know your business, but you're also suffering through immeasurable loss. My perspective changed significantly after watching a brilliant TED Talk by Tilak Mandadi, former Executive Vice President of Digital Experiences at Disney Parks, Experiences and Products (the organization I currently work for). In his talk, he shares that he actually benefitted by getting back into his routine—going back to work, participating in his normal hobbies and activities—after tragedy struck his family (Mandadi 2020).

Tilak's empathy advocacy began when he tragically lost his daughter in 2017. At nineteen years old, Cayley Mandadi was allegedly raped and murdered by her boyfriend. The beating was so bad that Cayley was barely recognizable when she arrived at the hospital. After Tilak made his way through the painful experience of putting his daughter to rest, he was left with a big decision: should he return to work? (Mandadi 2020).

While it was challenging, Tilak has been glad that he returned, finding the experience therapeutic, and feels that his coworkers have benefited as well.

"When you lose the most precious thing in your life, you gain a lot of humility, and a very different perspective free of egos and agendas, and I think I'm a better coworker and a leader because of that."

I also believe that my husband Jon is a better coworker, leader, and all-around person because of what he went through. To Tilak's point, when you lose the thing most precious to you, you gain gratitude for every moment you have and resilience to get through the tough ones.

Tilak mentions how important empathy training is for employees in order to foster support. I would go a step further and say that all of us, working or not, should go through empathy training. I think of the countless challenging conversations my husband has had with people who just didn't know what to say after 9/11. I think of the countless challenging conversations I've had with people who don't understand the complexities of infertility.

And while learning empathy in childhood does help, hope is not lost for adults who struggle to empathize. A study by Emily Teding van Berkhout and John M. Malouff shows that empathy can be taught and developed through proper training. (Teding van Berkhout & Malouff 2016). Just like any practice, empathy can become muscle memory and a more organic response to others.

While most of the empathy training we see out there is designed for businesses, the benefits of empathy in our lives are clear. According to Dr. Jeremy Sutton, having empathy can improve how we see ourselves and others, work relationships, marriages, parenting, and global relations (Sutton 2020).

"Psychologist Robert Ornstein and biologist Paul Ehrlich, in *Humanity on a Tightrope* (2012), point out that while we are hardwired to empathize with those closest to us, by extending humanity's compassion, we will be able to tackle the challenges ahead, from global warming to pandemics and war" (Sutton 2020).

Could greater empathy have saved us from 9/11? And, while empathy might not be able to prevent a pandemic, could it have made the situation less divisive than the one we see ourselves in now?

Tilak didn't choose his tragedy. Neither did my husband, and I certainly did not choose to be infertile. But because of it, we are better leaders who can advocate for empathy training. As the 9/11 Surviving Children are now in the workforce, they too can be advocates for change. The same can be said for anyone who has experienced grief and hasn't found that their community supports a safe place to bring their full selves. The empathy you gain as you walk through life's most challenging times can become your superpower to shape the way you live and work.

The challenge with empathy is that it is an emotion. It is difficult to *make* people feel something when they don't. What's more important are the actions they take regardless of how they feel. As a part of solid empathy training, attendees are taught what the differences between active and passive listening are and how we can implement the former more often. Activities could also include pairing folks who are total strangers and from completely different backgrounds. The exercise would organically allow each participant to learn more about people whose perspectives differ greatly from your own.

I've found that these practices have really helped me, especially at work. There are countless times when I work with partners whose roles and perspectives I do not fully understand. Even with a general idea of how we work together, there are many times where I've asked myself, "Why is this so hard?" or "What are they doing all day?" The irony is not lost on me that I ask them for grace and empathy when I present them with a roadblock as well.

Instead of quickly going to this place of judgment, I began scheduling one-on-one time with these folks. I asked them to give me a glimpse into their day-to-day lives, from their work responsibilities to who they are as a person. What are their likes? Dislikes? What can I do to make things easier on them? How do they prefer to work and be communicated with?

What I found by doing this is that we have way more in common than we don't—and even the differences, I found fascinating. I was able to be a better advocate for these partners because I actively listened to their challenges. Now I feel these partners have my back, and vice versa. It was difficult to step out in faith and take a chance on these methods, but they *really* work. Turns out that other people are humans too with complex backgrounds and experiences, just like us.

THE FUTURE IS BRIGHT

As someone who is currently going through the worst year of my life, the 9/11 Surviving Children have taught me a great deal about dealing with my grief and trauma.

I thought I'd be able to end this book with an easy summary of how others can cope with their challenges. I even hoped that, by the end of this book, I'd be able to tell you that I'm now pregnant and all of my problems are solved. After all, we live in the age of BuzzFeed articles, where we all just want ten easy steps to heal ourselves. The 9/11 Surviving Children's reflections required time—twenty years of it to be exact. As I currently live in the middle of my struggle, I recognize that time isn't something I've given myself yet. While it's not easy to look back after twenty years, it comes with a certain level of perspective that isn't possible after one year, or even ten.

If you are like me and in the middle of your struggle, I hope that this encourages you that even if you aren't able to be reflective about your challenge right now, you will someday be on the other side and looking back. It just takes time, which is something that can't be taught, but rather experienced.

It might be too soon to reflect on how the COVID-19 pandemic has changed us, but I hope in twenty years we can look back and find that we are better people because of all we went through. Do we see the same bit of warmth and camaraderie amongst fellow man that we saw after 9/11? Or have we all lost something since then? A piece of our humanity? If we are lost, how can we find that unity again? What can we do with all of this unfortunate wisdom we've accumulated in the past twenty years? It may sound Pollyanna, but maybe the 9/11 Surviving Children got it right when they said that kindness is the key to a better world.

I believe that incredible community, parental role modeling, therapeutic techniques, renewed appreciation for life, spirituality, and time are ingredients that have helped many 9/11 Surviving Children become thriving adults. For many, it is not because they lost their parent, but because they had their parents in the first place, that made them who they are.

Reflecting when you're in the middle of a tragedy is not easy. I'm experiencing that myself as I try to find joy on days where it seems there is none. But we do have history to remind us of the possibilities. After the Spanish Flu epidemic of 1918 came the roaring twenties. After 9/11 came the unity of our nation we had never seen before. If we've learned anything from the 9/11 Surviving Children, it's that time and kindness can do wonders. There was a time after 9/11 where people embraced without inhibition. Where just one look at a fellow driver or pedestrian could communicate what we all were thinking and feeling. If we can learn to lead with our hearts again, empathize with others, and give ourselves grace, there is no stopping us.

The 9/11 Surviving Children have so much to give us, even after having so much taken away from them. Some will go on to lead businesses and raise families with a unique perspective on life. They have a resiliency that is born from the remains of their tragedy. Like a phoenix, they've risen from the ashes of the trauma to find great triumph. They are still here, standing tall, pushing forward, and making the most of each day.

My greatest hope for this book is that we use these stories to guide our own paths, find the techniques that work for us, and advocate for empathy training in our communities. We have a great opportunity, here and now, to ask for what we need most. After all, it's only **together** that we will rise.

In an effort to bring this call to action to life, I've created the Rise Together community. The mission of this group stands to provide a safe space for others to share their stories of triumph. As we grow, the hope is to play an active role in communities, providing boots-on-the-ground resources and empathy training. Doing so will better equip current and future generations with the skills to face the highs and lows of life.

The challenge with a book is that once it's printed and the ink has dried, changes are challenging to make. The opportunity with our Rise Together community is that it will forever be a dynamic space that grows with the people it serves. I hope you'll join us as we take these stories off the pages and into our world. You can find us on Facebook by searching "Rise Together—The Rise From the Ashes Community."

I have no doubt these 9/11 Surviving Children and all those they impact are going to roar their way out of this pandemic and into a better and brighter future for all. But the journey doesn't end with this book. I believe that this is just the beginning for all of us. We should not let the 9/11 Surviving Children stand alone. We cannot. It's our turn now to let their stories be the fuel that lights the fire under our own revivals. So, what are you waiting for? Get out of here! You've got some rising to do!

ACKNOWLEDGEMENTS

———

I'd like to acknowledge those who have given this book, and the stories within it, legs strong enough to move forward:

The Lynch Family, The Kuritz Family, Matthew Bocchi, Anne Nelson, The Thomas Family, Rebecca Asaro, The Burnett Family, Nicole Foster, Maria Garcia, Alexa Edwards, Cat Brennan, Stacie Boyar, K Thomas, everyone at The Tuesday's Children Organization, Eric Koester, Rebecca Bruckenstein, Mike Butler, Dr. Sue McGorry, Bety Teigeiro and Erick Iglesias, Thea Trinidad Budgen (Zelina Vega), and Pete Davidson.

I'd also like to gratefully acknowledge:

Joyce Lino, Nancy Broadbent, Christopher White, Kathy Bonsell, Kristy Strobl, Judy Robinson, Mistie Poor, Caitlin Druckenmiller-Parades, Mary Catherine, Martha Lovell, Lori Turney, Jacqui Hatch, Laurie Wallace Theisen, Maria Elena Rumayor, Cassie Bax, Dan Villanti, Marissa Willman, Angelica MacQueen, Chloe Smith, Jennifer Mitchell, Chris Todd, Betsy Vargas, Crystal Schmitz, Kelly Curry, Sarah

Wilkinson, Megan Prine, Ashley Cruse, The George Family, Seth Fenstermaker, Jill Skiles, Megan McCormick, Erik Hoard, Kay Caprez, Megan Lione, Suzy Martinez, Laura Kicska, Joanna Keichel, David Finz, William Hudak, Eileen McAuliffe, Christy Keating, Reagan Hull, The Ingram Family, Britney Amore, Sandy Csizmar, Joyce Baltazar, Michelle Ruchalski, Michelle Saldivar, Karen Walczer, Charles Sherry, Bethany Eisenhart, Karla Quintanilla, The Meckes Family, The Rodrigues Family, Michelle Lynch, Jason Pasacreta, Leah Jeromin, Christopher Moore, AngelaRae Davis, Elaine Fink, The Teff Family, Joan Buttafuoco, Jennifer Marr, David B. Snyder Jr., Sara Wingerath-Schlanger, Lisa Zwikl, Susan Kittle, Amy Eberling, Desmond Dunham, Michelle Levene, Taylor Mills, Sandy Newman, Marty Plevel, James J. Gallagher, Seth Walker, Amanda Scherer, Jacqui Lyon, Brittany Lopez, Dakota Boles, Ron Lino, Johanna A. Kornberger, Kellyanne Ward, Jessie Cheng, Caitlyn Cody, Sarah Shear, Taylor VanDuyn, Greg Schumsky, Meredith McGarr, Nicole Lane, Ashtynn Allen, Natalie Bader, Casandra Magliane, Rebecca Asaro, Von Asuque, George Borcherding, Jane Albright, Kadie Rademaker, Kelly Hahnel, Sydney Sherrier, Shelly Hafler, Jason and Tracey Billig, Okasana Wittbrodt, Sydney Sherrier, Gianna Lopresti, Michelle Hernandez, Heather Marshall, Amy Costa, Becky Randazzo, Tracy O'Quinn, Kelly Falone, Corine van de Water, Cynthia Ward, Victoria Velez, Carlo Mahfouz, Mary Reitz, Yasemin Aksoy, Mary Reitz, Gwen Vigorito, Heather Lynn, Jessyca Cruciani, Charlene McGuckin, Sophia Montoya, Shabman Staebler, Brittany Dye, Kristin Guillemette, Ashley Brewer, Fernando Perdomo-Connot, Ashley Kreh, Bruno Arnese, Caitlyn Faison, Liza Quiles, Melissa East, Sue McGorry, John Brown, The Harvey Family, Elizabeth Van Beek, Melissa Logue, Amanda Clauser,

Kathleen Murray, Ian Tomesch & Mark Saylor, Karen Boylan, Ellen Sawin, The Davenport Family, Karen Hershey, Nichole Novak, Mary McCauley, Kimberly Waterman, Linda Helck, Carrie Yocum, Abbi Walsh, Gemma Miers, Megan Wagner, Sherry McCauley, Rebecca Bruce, Margaret Mosely, Stacy Reehl, Maria Salerno, Ashley Burke, Lisa Clarke, Rebecca Weaver, Heather Kattelman, Paula Ann Sandritter, Wendy Gray, Alyssa Fink, Mary E. Spence, Shalyn Leigh, Jessica Ormiston, Janet Brindle Reddick, Emiliano Alvarez, Day Rivera, Sharon Hoole, Michelle Carvallo, Christine Lino, Sarah Brame, Colleen Dorsey, Joey Lee, Lisa Godshall, Rachel Deluga, Sarah Pogge, Josephine Maida, David Sanchez, Laura Johnson, Janet Schadler, Bonnie Kreil, Patricia Curry, Jean Collins, Tyler Haney, Barbara Hile, Barbara Cotter, Robert Edelman, Karen Scott, Amy Morrell, Kjerstyna Davis, The Zimmer Family, Barbara Todd, Mercedes Newman, James Dvorak, Lisa Kingery, Donna Entrichel, Joseph Casciotti, Tammy Swanson, Carlos Navas, Kaitlin Ashleigh, Eva Fox, The Zirfas Family, Deborah Lynch-Jenkins, Mary Syslo, Monica L. Zink, Hansel Junior Ospino Orella, Kyle Martin Cohick, Jennifer Cilia, The Barrett Family, The Smith Family, Karen Kreh, Scott Quackenbush, Lauren Skinner, Anneliese Smith, Juan Carvajal, Robyn Petrie, Sierra Fisher and Spencer Palm, Tracey Hildebeidel, Gregory Lanning, Kendria Johnson, Christopher Kaelin, and Francisco Boden.

APPENDIX

——

INTRODUCTION

Vroman, Christina. "Interact With Us: Trauma and Positive Outcomes." Intercommunity Action. December 06, 2018. Accessed June 12, 2021. https://intercommunityaction.org/interact-us-trauma-positive-outcomes/.

THE DAY

Bocchi, Matthew John. Sway. Post Hill Press, 2021.

Boon, Jon. "WWE Star Vega's Father Died in 9/11 Terrorist Attacks on the World Trade Center." *The US Sun*. September 11, 2020. Accessed May 09, 2021. https://www.the-sun.com/sport/1456572/zelina-vega-father-9-11-death-terror-attack/.

Lanford, Marilyn. "Family Finds a Way through Grief to a Legacy of Hope." *Arkansas Catholic* - October 29, 2014. November 03, 2014. Accessed May 17, 2021. https://www.arkansas-catholic.org/news/article/4032/Family-finds-a-way-through-grief-to-a-legacy-of-hope.

Meyjes, Toby. "The 9/11 Kids Who Grew up without Their Parents." *Metro*. December 11, 2019. Accessed May 09, 2021. https://metro.co.uk/2016/09/11/the-911-kids-who-grew-up-without-their-parents-6117805/.

Murphy, Jan. "Jan Murphy." Chinlockcom. October 28, 2013. Accessed May 09, 2021. http://www.chinlock.com/2013/10/thea-trinidad-triumph-and-tragedy/.

Siemaszko, Corky. "COVID-19 Has Killed Dozens of 9/11 First Responders." NBCNews.com. September 11, 2020. Accessed May 09, 2021. https://www.nbcnews.com/news/us-news/covid-19-has-killed-dozens-9-11-first-responders-n1239885.

Texas A&M College of Medicine. "Psychiatrist Explains How the Brain Blocks Memory to Help Get through Traumatic Event." News Medical Life Science. June 19, 2019. Accessed May 09, 2021. https://www.news-medical.net/news/20161209/Psychiatrist-explains-how-the-brain-blocks-memory-to-help-get-through-traumatic-event.aspx.

Waichman, Parker. "Fatalities of the 9/11 Terrorist Attacks: Then and Now." Parker Waichman LLP. December 04, 2020. Accessed May 09, 2021. https://www.yourlawyer.com/library/911-terrorist-attacks-fatalities/.

THE STORIES

Lanford, Marilyn. "Family Finds a Way through Grief to a Legacy of Hope." *Arkansas Catholic* - October 29, 2014. November 03, 2014. Accessed May 09, 2021. https://www.arkansas-catholic.

org/news/article/4032/Family-finds-a-way-through-grief-to-a-legacy-of-hope.

NY Mag. September 11 by Numbers. September 2014. Accessed June 12, 2021. https://nymag.com/news/articles/wtc/1year/numbers.htm.

Unbound Medicine. "Safety and Comfort." Psychological First Aid (PFA). April 8, 2020. Accessed May 09, 2021. https://relief.unboundmedicine.com/relief/view/PTSD-National-Center-for-PTSD/1230001/all/Safety_and_Comfort.

THE TRAUMA

Bocchi, Matthew John. Sway. Post Hill Press, 2021.

Factual. "Children of 9/11" May 11, 2019. Video, 1:12:23. https://www.youtube.com/watch?v=uTZcTRGqjBo

Greenberg, David M., Simon Baron-Cohen, Nora Rosenberg, Peter Fonagy, and Peter J. Rentfrow. "Elevated Empathy in Adults following Childhood Trauma." PLOS ONE. October 3, 2018. Accessed June 12, 2021. https://journals.plos.org/plosone/article?id=10.1371/journal.pone.0203886.

Juzwiak, Rich. "Pete Davidson." Interview Magazine. April 13, 2018. Accessed May 09, 2021. http://www.interviewmagazine.com/culture/pete-davidson/.

Murphy, Jan. "Jan Murphy." Chinlockcom. October 28, 2013. Accessed May 09, 2021. http://www.chinlock.com/2013/10/thea-trinidad-triumph-and-tragedy/.

Roberts, Joe. "The King of Staten Island: What Happened To Pete Davidson's Father In Real Life." ScreenRant. June 16, 2020. Accessed June 12, 2021. https://screenrant.com/king-staten-island-pete-davidson-dad-fire-what-happened/.

Tominey, Shauna L., Elisabeth C. O'Byron, Susan E. Rivers, and Sharon Shapses. "Teaching Emotional Intelligence in Early Childhood." NAEYC. March 2017. Accessed May 09, 2021. https://www.naeyc.org/resources/pubs/yc/mar2017/teaching-emotional-intelligence.

BLACK CLOTHS

Idov, Michael. "Unidentified Remains - 9/11 Encyclopedia - September 11 10th Anniversary – NYMag - Nymag." *New York Magazine.* August 27, 2011. Accessed May 09, 2021. https://nymag.com/news/9-11/10th-anniversary/unidentified-remains/.

Pengelly, Martin. "Families of 9/11 Victims Protest against Move of Remains to New York Museum." *The Guardian.* May 10, 2014. Accessed May 09, 2021. https://www.theguardian.com/world/2014/may/10/911-victims-families-protest-move-remains-new-york-museum.

COUNTING

Centers for Disease Control and Prevention. "Posttraumatic Stress Disorder in Children." Centers for Disease Control and Prevention. March 22, 2021. Accessed May 09, 2021. https://www.cdc.gov/childrensmentalhealth/ptsd.html.

Peterson, Sarah. "Effects." The National Child Traumatic Stress
 Network. June 11, 2018. Accessed May 09, 2021. https://
 www.nctsn.org/what-is-child-trauma/trauma-types/com-
 plex-trauma/effects.

THE SIGNS

Pietrangelo, Ann. "Understanding the Baader-Meinhof Phenomenon." Healthline. December 17, 2019. Accessed June 12, 2021.
 https://www.healthline.com/health/baader-meinhof-phenom-
 enon#what-it-is.

Williams, Litsa. "16 Tips for Continuing Bonds with People We've
 Lost." Whats Your Grief. April 12, 2021. Accessed June 02,
 2021. https://whatsyourgrief.com/16-practical-tips-continu-
 ing-bonds/.

POSTTRAUMATIC GROWTH

March For Our Lives. "Mission & Story." March For Our Lives.
 September 17, 2020. Accessed June 12, 2021. https://marchforo-
 urlives.com/mission-story/.

THE TRIUMPH

CNN. "Sandy Hook Elementary Shooting: What Happened?"
 CNN. 2012. Accessed June 12, 2021. https://www.cnn.com/
 interactive/2012/12/us/sandy-hook-timeline/index.html.

FINDING MY OWN TRIUMPHS

"About Us." The Dinner Party. Accessed June 03, 2021. https://www.thedinnerparty.org/about.

Corrigan, Patricia. "How the Arts Can Ease Grief After Loss." Next Avenue. April 30, 2020. Accessed June 03, 2021. https://www.nextavenue.org/arts-ease-grief-after-loss/.

Enayati, Amanda. "The Importance of Belonging." CNN. June 01, 2012. Accessed June 03, 2021. https://www.cnn.com/2012/06/01/health/enayati-importance-of-belonging/index.html.

Gains, Ethical. "7 Reasons Adults Should Have Stuffed Animals Too." Bunnies By The Bay. December 11, 2020. Accessed June 02, 2021. https://bunniesbythebay.com/blogs/how-to-delight/7-reasons-adults-should-have-stuffed-animals-too.

Peele, Stanton. "The Stanton Peele Addiction Website." The Human Side Of Addiction: What Caused John Belushi's Death? April 1982. Accessed June 02, 2021. https://www.peele.net/lib/belushi.html.

Sloat, Sarah. "Why Humor Is So Effective as a Coping Strategy After Tragedy." Inverse. August 11, 2019. Accessed June 02, 2021. https://www.inverse.com/article/58452-how-to-use-humor-as-a-coping-strategy.

THE PRESENT

Edgers, Geoff. "Pete Davidson's Personal Life Always Overshadowed His Career. So He Turned It into a Movie." *The Washington Post*. June 10, 2020. Accessed June 05,

2021. https://www.washingtonpost.com/entertainment/
pete-davidsons-personal-life-always-overshadowed-his-
career-so-he-turned-it-into-a-movie/2020/06/10/2c81c79c-
a4e4-11ea-b473-04905b1af82b_story.html.

Low, Elaine. "Disney Increases Layoff Plans to 32,000 Employees
in First Half of 2021." Variety. March 04, 2021. Accessed June
03, 2021. https://variety.com/2020/TV/news/covid-19-impact-
walt-disney-business-1234840497/.

THE REAL INFLUENCERS

Buck, Chris, and Jennifer Lee. 2019. *Frozen II*. United States: Walt
Disney Studios Motion Pictures.

Nation. "Mr. Rogers Post Goes Viral." PBS. December 18, 2012.
Accessed June 15, 2021. https://www.pbs.org/newshour/nation/
fred-rogers-post-goes-viral.

BOUNDARIES

Bergen, Peter. "What Were the Causes of 9/11?" *Prospect Magazine*. September 24, 2006. Accessed June 03, 2021. https://www.
prospectmagazine.co.uk/magazine/whatwerethecausesof911.

"Courage." Dictionary.com. Accessed June 15, 2021. https://www.
dictionary.com/browse/courage.

Eckel, Sara. "The Power of Boundaries." *Psychology Today*. January
14, 2019. Accessed June 03, 2021. https://www.psychologytoday.
com/us/articles/201910/the-power-boundaries.

Elflein, John. "U.S. COVID-19 Average Deaths by Day." Statista. February 16, 2021. Accessed June 03, 2021. https://www.statista. com/statistics/1109281/covid-19-daily-deaths-compared-to-all-causes/.

Garfin, Dana Rose. "How the Pain of 9/11 Still Stays With a Generation." *Observer*. September 11, 2016. Accessed June 03, 2021. https://observer.com/2016/09/how-the-pain-of-911-still-stays-with-a-generation/.

Patalay, Praveetha, and Suzanne H. Gage. "Changes in Millennial Adolescent Mental Health and Health-related Behaviours over 10 Years: A Population Cohort Comparison Study." OUP Academic. February 27, 2019. Accessed June 03, 2021. https:// academic.oup.com/ije/advance-article-abstract/doi/10.1093/ije/ dyz006/5366210?redirectedFrom=fulltext.

Trousdale, Gary, and Kirk Wise. 1996. The Hunchback of Notre Dame. United States: Buena Vista Pictures.

COURAGE
George, Bill. "Courage: The Defining Characteristic Of Great Leaders." Forbes. April 24, 2017. Accessed June 12, 2021. https:// www.forbes.com/sites/hbsworkingknowledge/2017/04/24/ courage-the-defining-characteristic-of-great-leaders/?sh=69987c6211ca.

INTO THE UNKNOWN
Sandberg, Sheryl. "How Women Can Negotiate for More." Lean In. 2021. Accessed June 05, 2021. https://leanin.org/negotiation.

EMPATHY FIRST

Mandadi, Tilak. "3 Ways Companies Can Support Grieving Employees." TED. October 2020. Accessed June 05, 2021. https://www.ted.com/talks/tilak_mandadi_3_ways_companies_can_support_grieving_employees?language=en.

Sutton, Jeremy. "Developing Empathy: 8 Strategies & Worksheets to Become More Empathic." PositivePsychology.com. October 12, 2020. Accessed June 05, 2021. https://positivepsychology.com/empathy-worksheets/.

Teding van Berkhout, E., & Malouff, J. M. The efficacy of empathy training: A meta-analysis of randomized controlled trials. *Journal of Counseling Psychology, 63*(1), 32–41. (2016). https://doi.org/10.1037/cou0000093

Made in USA - Crawfordsville, IN
27487_9781637304266
08.30.2021 1219